# NEW WORLD
# CHINESE
# COOKING

## BILL JONES & STEPHEN WONG

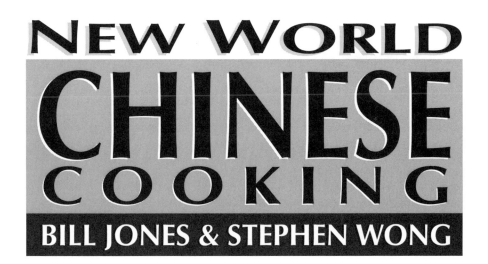

# NEW WORLD CHINESE COOKING

## BILL JONES & STEPHEN WONG

Robert ROSE

# NEW WORLD CHINESE COOKING

**For complete cataloguing data, see page 6.**

| | |
|---|---|
| DESIGN AND PAGE COMPOSITION: | MATTHEWS COMMUNICATIONS DESIGN |
| PHOTOGRAPHY: | MARK T. SHAPIRO |
| ART DIRECTION, FOOD PHOTOGRAPHY: | SHARON MATTHEWS |
| FOOD STYLIST: | KATE BUSH |
| PROP STYLIST: | MIRIAM GEE |
| MANAGING EDITOR: | PETER MATTHEWS |
| RECIPE EDITOR/TEST KITCHEN: | JUDITH FINLAYSON |
| INDEXER: | BARBARA SCHON |
| COLOR SCANS & FILM: | POINTONE GRAPHICS |

*Cover photo:* PAN-FRIED PORK CHOPS WITH SUN-DRIED TOMATOES AND CILANTRO
(PAGE 138)

Distributed in the U.S. by:
Firefly Books (U.S.) Inc.
P.O. Box 1338
Ellicott Station
Buffalo, NY   14205

Distributed in Canada by:
Stoddart Publishing Co. Ltd.
34 Lesmill Road
North York, Ontario
M3B 2T6

| ORDER LINES |
|---|
| Tel: (416) 499-8412 |
| Fax:(416) 499-8313 |

| ORDER LINES |
|---|
| Tel: (416) 445-3333 |
| Fax:(416) 445-5967 |

Published by: Robert Rose Inc. • 156 Duncan Mill Road, Suite 12
Toronto, Ontario, Canada  M3B 2N2   Tel: (416) 449-3535

Printed in Canada

12345678 BP 01 00 99 98

# CONTENTS

**Canadian Cataloguing in Publication Data**

Jones, W. A. (William Allen), 1959–
    New world Chinese cooking

Includes index.

ISBN 1-896503-70-5

1.  Cookery, Chinese.   I. Wong, Stephen, 1955– .   II. Title.

TX724.5.C5J66 1998        641.5951        C97-932608-9-0

# ACKNOWLEDGEMENTS

This book is a true team effort and bears truth to the saying that the end result is often greater than the sum of its parts. Many talented people have participated in the making of this book. In particular, the Robert Rose team of Bob Dees and Judith Finlayson illustrates the merits of perseverance and attention to detail. My extended family (including my wife Lynn and parents Bill and Joan) offered valuable advice and motivation for many of the recipes in this book. Friends and acquaintances in many countries have supported me, cooked for me, educated my palate and opened my mind to the wonderful world of food.

— Bill Jones

My gratitude and thanks to Ken Hom for his inspiration, generosity and friendship, and for taking the time out of his hectic schedule to write the wonderful foreword to this book.

A heartfelt thank you, once again, to all my friends and associates without whose continuing help, support and encouragement this book — or any others — would not have come into being: to Bill, my co-author, for his hard work, fabulous ideas and friendship; to Bob, Judith, Peter, Sharon, Mark, Kate and all the members of the production team for their respective talents, patience and hard work.; and last but not least, to my family for putting up with me through this whole process.

— Stephen Wong

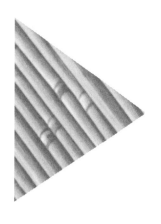

## PHOTO PROP CREDITS

The publisher and authors wish to express their appreciation to the following suppliers of props used in the food photography appearing in this book:

BOHEMEX LTD., TORONTO

HOMEFRONT, TORONTO

For those who feel that cooking is fuel
for the body and soul.

— W.A.J.


To my family and all my friends.
And to Jean Luc; may he now find peace.

— S.W.

# FOREWORD
## *by Ken Hom*

It is a curious fact that, until quite recently, many of us who cook did not exploit the diversity of seasonings, spices and food brought to the rest of the world by immigrants from China, Japan and Southeast Asia. Indeed, much of our cooking has remained persistently and traditionally North American — heavy on meat and mildly spiced. Still, given that food preferences are so deeply rooted in culture and psychology, the reluctance to experiment with new tastes and flavors is perhaps understandable.

Today, however, that reluctance is being rapidly over-come. Cooking in many North American kitchens is being revitalized, and is demonstrating a remarkable openness to (and acceptance of) many new ingredients, flavors, and techniques. There is a growing trend which, in the early 1980s, I described as "East/West cuisine" or, if you wish, "fusion cuisine." It is a cooking style that emphasizes the blending of foods, spices, flavorings and techniques that, historically, have evolved in isolation from one another. The introduction and acceptance of Asian influences which began in California has now spread to other cities throughout the world, including New York, London, Vancouver and Sydney — even back to Hong Kong. And this is due in large part, perhaps, to the growing spread of Asian immigrants to Europe, America and Australia.

Many of these recent arrivals have opened restaurants and food stores specializing in Asian cuisine, and featuring foods and ingredients totally unlike the chow mein or egg foo young dishes formerly offered in many cheap restaurants. In the process, they have educated and delighted the western palate. Coverage of the new cuisines has appeared in cookbooks, magazines, newspapers and on television. Specialty shops and supermarkets, responding to consumer demand, now stock foods and ingredients that, only a few years ago, were virtually unknown in North America. And now words such as stir-fry, bean curd, tofu, wok, sushi and bok choy are firmly established in our culinary lexicon.

Stephen Wong and Bill Jones, through their books and other writings, have championed this fusion style of cooking. Their *New World Chinese Cooking* is filled with imaginative and creative recipes that reflect honest cooking — simple, quick, healthy and easy to prepare. Their mouth-watering recipes are full of inspiring combinations. These are dishes that are both familiar and exotic, as well as delightfully satisfying. It is obvious through this bold and unique cookbook that Stephen and Bill have accomplished their goal of merging cuisines to create something new and innovative, while preserving links to ancient culinary traditions. I look forward to trying every single delicious recipe, as I know you will.

— *Ken Hom*

# INTRODUCTION

Easy to prepare, delicious to eat and inspiring a sense of culinary adventure —- that's the essence of our East-meets-West approach to Chinese cooking. Although our principal intention is to capture the flavors and textures of the finest Chinese cooking, we've also worked hard to ensure that the recipes in this book are easy to produce in the average North American kitchen.

A quick glance will tell you that while the roots of our recipes extend to traditional Chinese cooking, they are often animated by techniques and flavor combinations associated with other cuisines. Because our primary objective was to make our recipes both accessible and delicious, we've used readily available ingredients and employed simple techniques that require only ordinary tools and equipment. On the rare occasions when we've used ingredients that may be less familiar — which, incidentally we've done because we believe you'll enjoy the sense of discovery associated with their use — we've provided commonplace substitutions.

Today, "fusion", which defines our mix-and-match approach to cooking, is a trendy term in culinary circles. But fusion is simply a contemporary take on an age-old process. And like all cuisines, Chinese cooking is constantly evolving. As new ingredients from different parts of the world have become available and affordable, Chinese chefs have adapted to incorporate them into their repertoire. For instance, the unique combination of spices in Indonesian satay sauce has long been a signature feature in the regional cooking of Chiu Chow, a province along China's southeastern coast. Today, Japanese-inspired *sashimi* (made from salmon, tuna, lobster or geoduck) occupies a prominent place on menus in Chinese restaurants around the world. Our East-meets-West collaboration falls firmly into this well-established tradition and we hope it will encourage you to explore the cornucopia of possibilities hiding in your own pantry.

**BILL JONES**

**STEPHEN WONG**

# THE CHINESE PANTRY

Broadly speaking, the fundamentals of Chinese cooking fall into two categories: tools and techniques; and ingredients and flavorings. In this chapter, we've included a brief summary of those fundamentals. Other comments can be found in the marginalia adjacent to each recipe.

## TOOLS

### The wok

Basically, you won't require any special equipment to make the recipes in this book. That said, we'd like to sing the praises of that wonderful Chinese invention, the wok. A wok with a tight-fitting dome-shaped lid is an extremely versatile tool which can be used to cook practically anything. Because it has a rounded bottom and sloping sides, it has a larger surface for stir-frying. The wok is also great for deep-frying — better than a traditional frying pan. It's also great for shallow frying, poaching, braising or steaming. The heavier the wok, the better it is for the purposes of heat retention. And with heatproof handles, a wok can double as a roasting pan. For stove-top use, traditional woks require an adapter ring, although many woks on the market today have a large enough flat bottom to be placed directly on the element.

### The electric rice cooker

At the opposite end of the versatility spectrum, this device is the only "luxury" kitchen equipment we recommend. It exists for only one purpose— to make perfect rice. Since most of the recipes in this book are designed to be served in the format of a traditional Chinese meal — with one or more dishes of vegetables and meats accompanied by a serving of fluffy steamed rice — the electric rice cooker takes the guesswork out of making this all-important staple.

### A good knife

If there's one activity that characterizes Chinese cooking, it's chopping. To make your work easier, we recommend that you purchase a good stainless steel chef's knife — it's a lifetime investment. But inexpensive Chinese or Japanese vegetable cleavers, preferably made from stainless steel, also work very well.

# TECHNIQUES

The techniques described below are probably familiar to you since, to varying degrees, they're also used in other cuisines. This simple glossary is meant to summarize how some common techniques are used in the context of this book.

One of the principal factors in the evolution of Chinese cooking techniques is China's long history of chronic fuel shortages. Consequently, Chinese food is typically cooked very quickly — stir-frying, for example — or very slowly over low heat. Techniques such as steaming were also developed to accommodate this culture of scarcity. It's not uncommon, even today, to find large cooking pots containing dishes of food that are being steamed simultaneously with the rice that will accompany the meal. But times are changing. And as fuel availability becomes less of a problem, methods such as deep frying are gaining in popularity in China.

### Blanching

Blanching is the technique of briefly boiling an ingredient in water, which may or may not be salted. The process ensures that hard vegetables (carrots or squash, for example), which are intended for a quick-cooking process such as stir-frying, will be properly cooked. Blanching can also be used to wilt or soften ingredients like chives or green onions if special presentations such as tying fish rolls is involved. In the case of green vegetables, blanching should always be followed by immediate cooling in ice water; this prevents overcooking and discoloration.

## Braising

Braising is the process of cooking food slowly over low heat in a covered pan with a small amount of stock or flavored liquid. It is an excellent way to prepare tougher cuts of meat or for infusing flavors into an otherwise bland ingredient such as tofu. Meat and poultry is often browned first, then simmered slowly in the braising liquid. Braising can be done on the stovetop or in a moderate oven. After the food is cooked, the volume of braising liquid is usually reduced, or thickened with starch, to create a rich sauce.

## Cutting and chopping

As we've mentioned, many Chinese recipes are cooked quickly, so ingredients need to be prepared in advance. We recommend having all the ingredients for a recipe chopped or sliced before you begin to cook. Occasionally, specific cutting instructions are given in our recipes to enhance presentation. Vegetables or meats should be cut in ways that make use of their individual characteristics, as well as to ensure that they will cook evenly. For example, meat is often sliced across the grain. In addition to ensuring that it takes little time to cook, this also maximizes tenderness. When herbs and seasonings are described as minced, this usually means that the item is cut into thin slices or threads then chopped until a coarse meal is obtained. This ensures that the ingredient releases its flavors faster during cooking. Vegetables are cut into bite-size segments for similar reasons. The finer you can slice or dice a product, the faster the cooking time and the more consistent the end result.

Sometimes you may come across an instruction to smash a clove of garlic, a piece of ginger root or a length of green onion. Smashing helps to release the flavor of ingredients that will be removed after the marinating or cooking is done.

### Deep-frying

This involves cooking pieces of food in oil, at moderately high temperatures. Deep-frying is a fast process that allows food to be cooked quickly on all sides at once. Often a starch crust or batter is used to isolate the food from the fat and to provide a crunchy exterior while retaining moisture and flavors. This lends texture to the food and it's an important component of Chinese cooking. The Chinese believe that good food must not only look, smell and taste good but should also excite our tactile senses.

### Poaching

Poaching is a gentle process wherein food is slowly cooked in a liquid just below the boiling point. The Chinese method of poaching is to bring the food and liquid to a boil and then turn off the heat — thus allowing the food to steep until it's cooked. A whole chicken or duck is often cooked this way. Poaching can produce wonderful silky-tender results, as is evident in the soya- or white-cooked chickens sold in Chinese barbecue shops.

### Roasting

This is a wonderful way to cook meats, crisp noodles, or to intensify flavors. The oven is usually set at a high temperature and the food is often coated with seasoning or, in some cases, a light film of oil to prevent burning and to promote coloring. Traditionally, in China, roasting is done mostly in restaurants and large kitchens where ovens are available. But in North America, virtually every household has an oven, so we've included recipes that take advantage of this fact.

### Steaming

Steaming is a common technique in Chinese cooking. It cooks food quickly while retaining nutrients and flavor. Most Chinese cooks use various sizes of bamboo or steel steamers. You can find them in Asian markets.

The steamer is placed in a wok containing boiling water. The quantity of water is such that it does not reach the

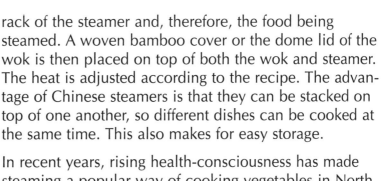

rack of the steamer and, therefore, the food being steamed. A woven bamboo cover or the dome lid of the wok is then placed on top of both the wok and steamer. The heat is adjusted according to the recipe. The advantage of Chinese steamers is that they can be stacked on top of one another, so different dishes can be cooked at the same time. This also makes for easy storage.

In recent years, rising health-consciousness has made steaming a popular way of cooking vegetables in North America. Most cookware sets now come with steamers which work on the same principle as their Chinese cousins. If you have one of these steamers, it can be used to cook our recipes in most cases, although some minor adaptations may be required. Just use your common sense.

Many kitchen shops sell round or square racks which fit into a wok. These have one advantage over traditional Chinese steamers since a dish containing the food to be steamed can be placed directly on the rack. This enables you to serve the food directly from the steamer, making the presentation considerably easier. You can achieve the same result by placing a rack, or even some Mason jar lids, on the bottom of a wok or large skillet with a lid. Cover with water and bring to a boil; arrange the food on a heatproof plate, set the plate on the rack, cover with the lid and steam until cooked. You could even use a covered roasting pan as a steamer, setting a heatproof serving plate on top of a couple of heatproof bowls.

### Stir-frying

This technique is very similar to sautéeing. Typically, oil is heated in a skillet or wok until it's very hot. (If you're particularly concerned that the food will stick, heat the skillet or wok until it's very hot, then add the oil and heat for about 30 seconds.) The ingredients, which should be cut into bite-sized pieces, are then added to the hot oil. If the ingredients cook too quickly, add a little liquid to the pan to lower the heat. This will prevent food from sticking or scorching. Be careful not to put too much food in the pan or it will stew instead of fry. Add ingredients in the order of the time they take to

cook. (For example, carrots will take longer than asparagus.) If necessary, cook vegetables and meats separately, then combine them toward the end to finish the dish.

## Thickeners

In Chinese cooking, cornstarch, rather than flour, is often used to thicken sauces. The thickening process helps to concentrate flavors and allows the sauce to cling to the food, which enhances its taste. Since cornstarch is translucent when cooked, it gives sauces an attractive sheen. In order to ensure smooth emulsion, the starch needs to be dissolved in cold water before it's added to any hot liquid.

## Pesto making

Contrary to popular belief, pesto is a technique, not a purée of basil, garlic, pine nuts and olive oil. It can be used to preserve any fresh herb and can be flavored with a wide variety of spices, nuts and oils.

In the past, people made pesto laboriously by hand using a mortar and pestle — hence the name, pesto. But today, with the introduction of the blender and food processor the task is greatly simplified. Although it is not a classic Chinese technique, the Chinese have been making sauces that resemble pesto for centuries. An example is the minced ginger and scallion oil that is so often served with poached chicken. (We've included our own version of this recipe in the book.) Pesto can easily be frozen and stored until needed. Try freezing it in an ice cube tray; remove when frozen and store in a sealed plastic bag in the freezer.

## Toasting

Since our recipes often call for toasted nuts, seeds or spices, here's one way to ensure good results. Place the nuts or seeds or spices in a dry sauté pan and heat over medium heat. Constantly stir and toss the pan until the contents just begin to turn golden. Remove the pan quickly from the heat and transfer to a plate to cool.

# CHINESE INGREDIENTS

### Chilies

Chilies are native to Central and South America and have been exported and integrated into cuisines around the world. Today, the Chinese not only produce chilies, they also make some of the best chili sauces on the market. Chinese regional cooking, from the province of Szechuan in particular, is known in North America for its fiery character which is chiefly achieved by the addition of chilies.

"The smaller the pepper the hotter" is a well-known and substantially accurate saying. Since the inner membrane and seeds supply most of the heat in chilies, removing them with a knife makes sense if you want to lessen the impact. If your skin is sensitive, wear rubber gloves when working with chilies and don't touch your eyes while handling them.

### Cilantro

This is the herb form of coriander. In appearance the plant resembles Italian parsley but is distinguishable by its attractive, robust aroma. We use it often in sauces and even more frequently as a garnish. Cilantro is often sold as "fresh coriander leaves."

### Garlic

Garlic, the king of seasonings, is widely used in cooking all over the world. In Chinese cooking, garlic is used whole, chopped, crushed, pickled and even smoked. It's a key ingredient in various prepared sauces, ranging from the popular black bean sauce to hoisin and chili paste. Cooking garlic reduces its flavor, astringency and aromatic properties. If you burn it, however, garlic will add an unpleasant bitterness to a dish. Since recent research has linked garlic to a number of health benefits, feel free to add more garlic to the recipes we've included, if you're so inclined.

### Ginger root

The fresh rhizome — not the dried powder — is mandatory in Chinese cooking. Like garlic, its spicy fresh flavor and aroma is indispensable to the flavor of Chinese food. It's widely available, and good for you — recent studies suggest that ginger helps to purify the blood and lower cholesterol. When buying ginger, look for "hands" that are plump, heavy and free of blemishes. Young ginger, which is cream colored — without the usual bronze skin — is milder and available in season. Both types will keep, refrigerated, in an airtight container, for 2 weeks.

### *Mirin*

*Mirin* is a Japanese sweetened rice wine which is used to add a sweet balance to marinades or sauces. It's usually available in Asian markets; if you can't locate it, sugar-sweetened *sake*, white wine or sherry are fine substitutes.

### *Shaoxing* wine

This rich, mellow-tasting rice wine is used widely in Chinese cooking and is available in Asian markets, although you'll sometimes have to ask for it as it's kept behind the counter. Dry sherry makes a fair substitute but white wine or *sake* will not work nearly as well.

### Star anise

This is the woody, star-shaped seed pod of a tree indigenous to southwestern China. It has a robust licorice flavor and aroma, and is one of the key ingredients of Chinese 5-spice powder. It is generally available in supermarkets with a well-stocked spice section, as well as in Asian markets.

### Szechuan peppercorns

These are actually not peppercorns (which are seeds), but dried reddish-brown berries of *fagara* — a relative of the prickly ash. They have a spicy, complex, slightly numbing flavor, and are among the most ancient seasonings used in Chinese cooking. For best results, toast them in a dry skillet before using. They're available in Asian markets.

### Pepper, black or white

Since whole peppercorns have more flavor than ground pepper, we recommend that you buy pepper in this form and grind it in a pepper mill just before use. White pepper is stronger and hotter than black pepper. Therefore, less is needed to season a dish.

### Tofu (Bean curd)

Tofu has been nourishing people for almost two millennia. It is made from yellow soybeans that have been soaked, ground, mixed with water and heated to solidify the soy proteins. The resulting curd is protein-rich, nutritious and inexpensive. Tofu comes in many forms — from soft and silky to firm and dense. The kind you buy depends upon the use to which it is being put. Always buy tofu as fresh as possible and use within a day or two of opening the package. Freshly made tofu is available in Chinese markets. Commercial tofu is widely available in health food stores and grocery stores.

### Vinegar

Vinegar is an important component of Asian cooking. For instance, it is used commonly in dishes containing sweet-and-sour sauce, among other things. White rice vinegar is a smooth mild vinegar which can be used effectively to balance hot and sweet flavorings. Darker rice vinegars come in black, red and dark brown versions, and are made from the fermentation of different varieties of rice. All Chinese vinegars are less acidic than western vinegars and impart unique flavors to dishes. They're most similar to balsamic vinegar, which can usually be used as a substitute.

# ASIAN VEGETABLES

### Chinese broccoli (Gailan)

This bright olive-green vegetable is highly nutritious and loaded with iron, calcium and vitamins A and C. The flavor is earthy and slightly bitter and is traditionally served, blanched, with a drizzle of oyster sauce on top. Substitute broccoli, rapini or kale.

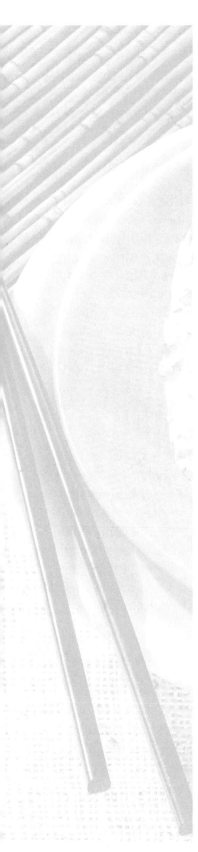

### Chinese mustard greens (Gai choy)

These greens, often called Chinese mustard cabbage, are used in stir-fries, soups and often preserved in a wide variety of forms — for instance, pickled, salted or fermented. Choose mustards that have firm and juicy stems and whole, unwilted leaves. Substitute arugula, spinach or rapini.

### Chinese green cabbage (*Sui choy* or Napa cabbage)

This soft green cabbage is often called Napa cabbage in North America. The mildly flavored leaves, which cook very quickly and reach their peak of flavor when barely wilted, are excellent in soups or lightly stir-fried. Finely sliced green or Savoy cabbage make good substitutes.

### Chinese white cabbage (Bok choy)

Many variants of Chinese white cabbage are sporadically available in North American markets. Bok choy, which is sold both as a mature vegetable and a young "baby" version, is one of the most common. Crunchy in texture and slightly bitter in taste, it has a thick white stem bordered by dark green leaves. Substitute Napa cabbage, Savoy cabbage or young kale.

### Chinese chives

Asian markets sell many types of chives, including yellow, flowering, garlic and green varieties. Choose chives that are firm and not wilted. Their pungent flavor adds a distinctive taste to most dishes in this book. If you can't find the Chinese version, garden chives or even green onion tops will do.

### Chinese mushrooms

The three types of dried Chinese mushrooms that we use in this book are commonly available in Asian markets:

***Dried black mushrooms***, often called by their Japanese name, *shiitake*, add texture and a robust flavor to dishes. The large ones, with a white cracked design on top, are the most highly valued, and can be expensive. Buy medium-priced ones for best flavor and value.

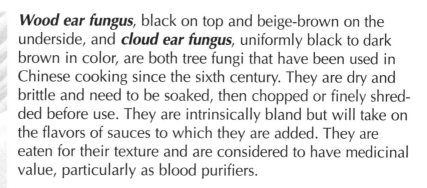

*Wood ear fungus*, black on top and beige-brown on the underside, and *cloud ear fungus*, uniformly black to dark brown in color, are both tree fungi that have been used in Chinese cooking since the sixth century. They are dry and brittle and need to be soaked, then chopped or finely shredded before use. They are intrinsically bland but will take on the flavors of sauces to which they are added. They are eaten for their texture and are considered to have medicinal value, particularly as blood purifiers.

## Green onions

These provide a distinctive taste and visual appeal. In some recipes, we specify using only the green or white parts of the onion; otherwise you can assume that the whole onion should be used.

## Prepared sauces and spice mixes

The prepared sauces called for in this book will help to establish the flavor profile of a dish without the fuss of making it from scratch. Although most of these sauces are widely available and are great time savers, they're not without a downside. The problem with using prepared sauces is that the contents and taste of different brands may vary quite dramatically. We suggest you experiment to find the one that best suits you.

*Black bean sauce.* Prepared black bean sauce, which is widely available in small glass jars, often with the addition of garlic, is another fermented and salted soybean product.

*Chili sauce.* There are many kinds of chili or hot sauce from around the world, including that old North American standby, Tabasco, and each has its own subtle flavor differences. Basically, they're used to add flavor and punch to a dish and usually should be used with caution since they're inclined to be fiery. The kind we use most often comes in a straight-sided bottle with a green top and is made in California. It's labeled Chili-Garlic Sauce. Again, taste and compare until you establish your preference.

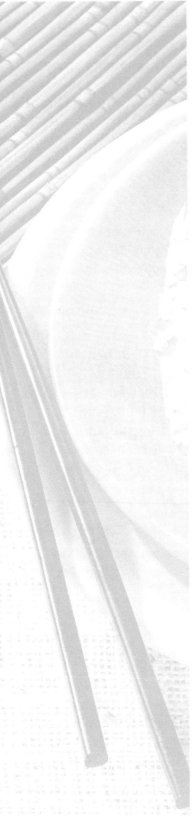

**Chili bean paste/sauce.** This spicy paste comes in many versions and in many brands but, basically, they're all composed of chilies, spices and a fermented soybean paste. They're used to add heat and flavor and they vary widely in taste and degree of spicing. Some varieties are extremely pungent and should be used with great restraint. Trial and, unfortunately, the odd error, will help you to find the brand you prefer and the quantity in which you like to use it.

**Curry powder.** In India, every region and village has its own variation of curry, which is actually a blend of spices, such as turmeric, cardamom, cinnamon and tamarind, rather than a single spice. Most commercial varieties are available in different strengths, ranging from mild to hot. Dry curry powder should be heated (preferably with oil) to release the flavors. Madras curry powder, which is available in Asian markets, is sweeter and less bitter than most commercial versions and we recommend its use in our recipes.

**Char Sui sauce** is the sweet-and-spicy paste that seasons Chinese barbecued pork. Its sweet flavor adds a pleasant and delicate element to dishes. It is especially good when the sweetness of the sauce is balanced with a little rice vinegar, creating a sweet-and-sour effect. It's widely available in Chinese markets but if you can't find it, barbecue sauce makes an acceptable substitute.

**Hoisin sauce.** Hoisin is another fermented soybean product, made from a combination of soya, garlic, vinegar, sugar and spices. This sweet-and-spicy paste is great with meat (especially pork and duck) and is used to flavor a variety of sauces and dips.

**Plum sauce.** This is a sweet, tart and spiced purée of plums, ginger, chili, spices, vinegar and sugar. Plum sauce varies widely in its consistency, sweetness, and level of spice. So, again, we recommend that you try several varieties to determine your favorite. It's a great addition to sauces and makes a wonderful glaze for roasted poultry, meats, seafood or vegetables. Try brushing it on roasted potatoes, then running them under the broiler.

## Oyster sauce

This ancient brew is made from boiling large vats of oysters, soya sauce, salt, spices and seasonings. Commercial preparations vary widely in salt and MSG content, and most contain modified cornstarch as a thickener. We recommend that you buy a premium version, which is usually available in Asian markets. It can be used right from the bottle as a dipping sauce to flavor vegetables — or used in cooking, where it adds a rich dimension to many dishes.

## Soya sauce

Soya sauce has been around for about 3,000 years. It's made from fermented, aged soybeans. Since some brands may contain flour, people with a gluten allergy should read labels carefully. Low-sodium and wheat-free versions are available.

We suggest experimenting with soya sauces to find a brand that suits your taste. It keeps indefinitely, even when stored at room temperature.

*Light soya sauce* is the least aged and the one most often used in cooking. Unless otherwise specified, when we call for soya sauce in our recipes, this is what we mean.

*Dark soya sauce*, slightly thicker and longer-aged than the lighter version, is preferred for dipping and braising. It's also widely available.

*Sweet soya sauce* (*kecap manis*) is made from fermenting soybean and cane sugar. Since it's more difficult to find, we've included a recipe for making your own substitute (see page 34).

# BASICS

# CHICKEN STOCK

**MAKES ABOUT
18 CUPS (4.5 L)**

*Basic chicken stock is
probably the best liquid
to add to any sauce —
whether meat-, fish- or
vegetable-based.*

*Chicken necks and
backs are usually avail-
able at the meat counter
of grocery stores.*

*The stock will keep
refrigerated for about
1 week or it can be
frozen and kept for up
to 2 months.*

| | | |
|---|---|---|
| 5 lb | chicken backs and necks | 2.5 kg |
| 3 | large onions, peeled and roughly chopped | 3 |
| 3 | carrots, roughly chopped | 3 |
| 3 | stalks celery, roughly chopped | 3 |
| Half | garlic head | Half |
| 8 | slices ginger root | 8 |
| 1 | small handful mixed herbs (cilantro, basil, etc.) | 1 |
| 5 | whole black peppercorns | 5 |
| 1 tbsp | salt (preferably sea salt) | 15 mL |
| 20 cups | water | 5 L |

1. Place ingredients in a large stockpot, adding more water, if necessary, to cover. Bring mixture to a boil; reduce heat and simmer gently for 3 hours, skimming occasionally to remove any foam or impurities that rise to the top. Try not to let the mixture boil or the broth will be cloudy.

2. Strain into a container and cool to room temperature before refrigerating. (If hot stock is placed directly in the fridge, it will sometimes sour.) For a more intensely flavored stock, let liquid cool; return stock to pot and, over low heat, simmer until volume is reduced by half.

# FISH STOCK

| | | |
|---|---|---|
| 5 lb | fish bones, rinsed under cold water to remove any blood | 2.5 kg |
| 3 | large onions, peeled and roughly chopped | 3 |
| 2 | leeks, washed and roughly chopped | 2 |
| 3 | celery stalks, roughly chopped | 3 |
| 1 | head fennel, diced | 1 |
| 3 | bay leaves | 3 |
| 1 | small handful mixed herbs (cilantro, basil, etc.) | 1 |
| 5 | whole black peppercorns | 5 |
| 2 tsp | fennel seed | 10 mL |
| 2 tsp | whole allspice | 10 mL |
| 2 tsp | whole coriander seed | 10 mL |
| 2 cups | white wine | 500 mL |
| 20 cups | water | 5 L |

*A good fish stock is clear and has a pleasant fish flavor. Acidity, in the form of wine or lemon juice, helps to make the stock clear.*

*Halibut, sole or other white-fleshed fish make the best stock.*

*Canned or bottled clam juice makes a good substitute for fish stock but be sure to tell your guests it's part of the recipe since it can trigger a reaction for people with shellfish allergies.*

*The stock will keep refrigerated for about 1 week or it can be frozen and kept for up to 2 months.*

1. Place ingredients in a large stockpot, adding more water, if necessary, to cover. Bring mixture to a boil; reduce heat and simmer gently for 1 hour, skimming occasionally to remove any foam or impurities that rise to the top. Try not to let the mixture boil or the broth will be cloudy.

2. Strain into a container and cool to room temperature before refrigerating. (If hot stock is placed directly in the fridge, it will sometimes sour.) For a more intensely flavored stock, let liquid cool; return stock to pot and, over low heat, simmer until volume is reduced by half.

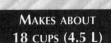

# BEEF STOCK

**MAKES ABOUT
18 CUPS (4.5 L)**

*Slowly roasting the
beef bones caramelizes
their sugars and enriches
this stock.*

*The stock will keep
refrigerated for about
a week or it can be
frozen and kept for up
to 2 months.*

**Preheat oven to 400° F (200° C)**
**Roasting pan**

| | | |
|---|---|---|
| 5 lb | beef bones (shin or neck), rinsed to remove any blood | 2.5 kg |
| 3 | large onions, peeled and roughly chopped | 3 |
| 3 | carrots, roughly chopped | 3 |
| 3 | stalks celery, roughly chopped | 3 |
| 1 | head garlic | 1 |
| 1/2 cup | tomato paste | 125 mL |
| 3 | bay leaves | 3 |
| 1 | small handful thyme | 1 |
| 1 | small handful rosemary | 1 |
| 1 | small handful marjoram | 1 |
| 1 | bunch parsley stalks | 1 |
| 5 | whole black peppercorns | 5 |
| 20 cups | water | 5 L |

1. Place bones in pan and roast until lightly golden, about 2 hours. Add vegetables and garlic; roast 1 hour. Add tomato paste, stirring to coat. Roast 30 minutes.

2. Place roasted bones and vegetables in a large stock pot; add remaining ingredients. Add more water, if necessary, to cover. Bring mixture to a boil; reduce heat and simmer 6 to 8 hours, skimming occasionally to remove any foam or impurities that rise to the top. Try not to let the mixture boil or the broth will be cloudy.

3. Strain into a container and cool to room temperature before refrigerating. (If hot stock is placed directly in the fridge, it will sometimes sour.) For a more intensely flavored stock, let liquid cool and remove any fat from the top; return stock to pot and, over low heat, simmer until volume is reduced by half.

*UPPER: BEEF TOMATO GARLIC SPRING ROLLS (PAGE 46)* ➤
*LOWER: CRAB AND CORN PANCAKES WITH A SWEET-AND-SOUR SAUCE (PAGE 38)*

# VEGETABLE STOCK

MAKES ABOUT
18 CUPS (4.5 L)

| | | |
|---|---|---|
| 3 | large onions, peeled and roughly chopped | 3 |
| 2 | leeks, washed and roughly chopped | 2 |
| 5 | stalks celery, roughly chopped | 5 |
| 5 | bay leaves | 5 |
| 1 | handful mixed herbs (cilantro, basil, etc.) | 1 |
| 10 | whole black peppercorns | 10 |
| Half | head garlic | Half |
| 2 | slices ginger root | 2 |
| 1 tsp | fennel seed | 5 mL |
| 1 tsp | allspice | 5 mL |
| 1 tsp | cilantro | 5 mL |
| 2 cups | white wine | 500 mL |
| 20 cups | water | 5 L |

*A good vegetable stock will add life to any soup or sauce.*

*Try using other vegetables such as parsnips, cabbages, fennel, kale, and cauliflower.*

*Roasting the vegetables first makes a nice brown stock which can be enhanced by adding 1 tbsp (15 mL) tomato paste.*

*The stock will keep, refrigerated, for about 1 week or it can be frozen and kept for up to 2 months.*

1. Place ingredients in a large stockpot, adding more water, if necessary, to cover. Bring mixture to a boil; reduce heat and simmer gently for 2 hours, skimming occasionally to remove any foam or impurities that rise to the top. Try not to let the mixture boil or the broth will be cloudy.

2. Strain into a container and cool to room temperature before refrigerating. (If hot stock is placed directly in the fridge, it will sometimes sour.) For a more intensely flavored stock, let liquid cool; return stock to pot and, over low heat, simmer until volume is reduced by half.

◄ ASPARAGUS GINGER SESAME CREAM SOUP (PAGE 55)

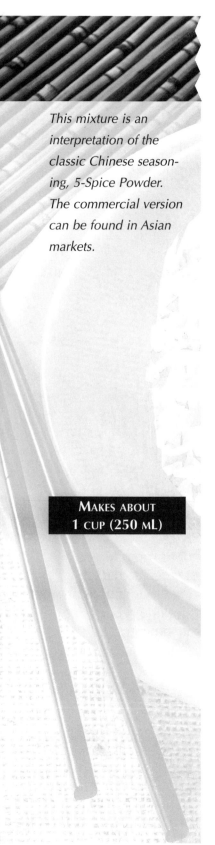

# HOME-STYLE 5-SPICE MIX

*This mixture is an interpretation of the classic Chinese seasoning, 5-Spice Powder. The commercial version can be found in Asian markets.*

| | | |
|---|---|---:|
| 2 tbsp | fennel seeds | 25 mL |
| 2 tbsp | clove sticks | 25 mL |
| 2 tbsp | star anise | 25 mL |
| 2 tbsp | Szechuan peppercorns | 25 mL |
| 2 | cinnamon sticks | 2 |

1. In a nonstick pan over medium-high heat, cook the spices, shaking the pan constantly. When the pan just begins to smoke, remove from heat. Transfer contents to a plate to cool.

2. In a small coffee or spice grinder (you can also use a mortar and pestle or blender or food processor), grind spices until a fine powder is obtained. Transfer to a small, sealable plastic container and reserve until needed.

**MAKES ABOUT
1 CUP (250 mL)**

# SWEET SOYA SAUCE SUBSTITUTE

| | | |
|---|---|---:|
| 1 cup | dark soya sauce | 250 mL |
| 2 tbsp | brown sugar | 25 mL |
| 1 tbsp | dark molasses | 15 mL |

1. Place ingredients in a small bowl; mix well to combine. Cover and store in refrigerator until needed.

*This pesto is a simple
mixture of green onions
laced with ginger and
melded together by
sesame seeds. It's
excellent on chicken
and makes a great
addition to soups and
salads or served over
plain rice.*

*The pesto keeps 1 week
in refrigerator.*

# GINGER GREEN ONION PESTO

| | | |
|---|---|---|
| 1 cup | sliced green onions | 250 mL |
| 2 tbsp | minced ginger root | 25 mL |
| 1 tsp | salt | 5 mL |
| 1 cup | vegetable oil | 250 mL |
| 1/2 cup | sesame seeds | 125 mL |

1. In a food processor or blender, combine all ingredients. Pulse on and off until the mixture achieves a uniform consistency. Transfer to a sealable container and refrigerate.

# TOASTED CHILI OIL

**MAKES ABOUT
2 CUPS (500 mL)**

Although chili peppers
were unknown in China
for much of its history
(they were imported
from Central America
only a few hundred
years ago), chili oil is
now a staple ingredient
in Chinese cooking.

This oil has a more pun-
gent , smoky flavor than
commercially available
varieties.

The oil will keep up
to 2 months in the
refrigerator.

| 2 tbsp | dried chili flakes | 25 mL |
| 2 cups | vegetable oil | 500 mL |

1. In a heavy skillet or small saucepan, heat chili
   flakes until toasted and almost smoking. Carefully
   pour in the oil and heat for 1 minute. Remove
   from heat and allow the flavors to infuse for at
   least 20 minutes.
2. Transfer to a sterilized glass jar or bottle and
   refrigerate.

# APPETIZERS

# CRAB AND CORN PANCAKES WITH SWEET-AND-SOUR SAUCE

**SERVES 4**

*Pancakes make versatile appetizers. This version marries a Chinese sweet-and-sour sauce with a New England-style corn and crabcake. The combination of butter and oil for frying helps to achieve a rich, golden brown finish.*

**Preheat oven to warm**

## Sauce

| | | |
|---|---|---|
| 1 cup | tomato juice | 250 mL |
| 2 tbsp | brown sugar | 25 mL |
| 2 tbsp | rice vinegar | 25 mL |
| 1 tbsp | minced ginger root | 15 mL |
| 1 tbsp | grated horseradish | 15 mL |
| 1 tsp | cornstarch dissolved in 2 tbsp (25 mL) cold water | 5 mL |
| 1 tbsp | chopped cilantro | 15 mL |

## Pancakes

| | | |
|---|---|---|
| 4 oz | fresh or canned crab meat | 125 g |
| 1 cup | fresh or frozen corn kernels | 250 mL |
| 2 | large eggs, lightly beaten | 2 |
| 2 tbsp | cream *or* milk | 25 mL |
| 6 tbsp | all-purpose flour | 90 mL |
| 2 tsp | baking powder | 10 mL |
| | Salt and pepper to taste | |
| 1 tbsp | vegetable oil | 15 mL |
| 1 tbsp | butter | 15 mL |

1. In a small saucepan over medium-high heat, combine tomato juice, brown sugar, rice vinegar, ginger root and horseradish. Reduce heat to simmer; add dissolved cornstarch and stir until thickened. Add cilantro; mix well. Remove from heat and set aside.

2. In a mixing bowl, combine crab and corn. Add eggs, cream (or milk), flour and baking powder. Season to taste with salt and pepper. Mix well.

3. In a nonstick skillet, heat oil and butter over medium-high heat. Spoon batter into the pan to make 4 pancakes, each 2 inches (5 cm) in diameter. Cook 2 to 3 minutes per side or until golden. Keep warm. Repeat cooking procedure until all the batter is used up. Serve warm topped with sauce.

# GRILLED MUSSELS WITH SWEET PEPPERS IN SATAY GLAZE

*In this recipe, cherrystone clams or oysters are as appealing as mussels — simply steam until the shells open and remove the meat from the shells. You can also use scallops or fish fillets (use salmon or any other firm-fleshed fish), cut into bite-sized chunks.*

**Preheat broiler or start barbecue at medium-high heat**

| | | |
|---|---|---|
| 16 to 24 | large mussels | 16 to 24 |
| 1 | red bell pepper, cut into bite-size cubes | 1 |
| 1 | green pepper, cut into bite-size cubes | 1 |
| 8 | 5-inch (12.5 cm) wooden skewers, soaked in water for 4 hours | 8 |

**Satay glaze**

| | | |
|---|---|---|
| 1 tbsp | satay sauce (Chinese barbecue sauce) | 15 mL |
| 1 tbsp | soya sauce | 15 mL |
| 1 tbsp | honey | 15 mL |
| 1 tbsp | chicken stock | 15 mL |
| 1 tbsp | cider vinegar *or* rice vinegar | 15 mL |

1. In a large steamer or heavy-bottomed saucepan with a lid, steam mussels until they open. (Discard any that do not open.) Remove meat and set aside. Discard shells.

2. Thread mussel meat alternately with red and green pepper pieces onto prepared wooden skewers to form attractive brochettes.

3. In a small saucepan or microwaveable bowl, combine ingredients for glaze. Over low heat or in a microwave, cook until honey is dissolved. Stir to combine.

4. Lightly oil rack on barbecue or broiler. Baste mussel-pepper skewers evenly with glaze. Grill skewers, turning every 30 seconds or so to prevent burning. Baste frequently with remaining glaze. When cooked (about 4 minutes in total), transfer skewers to platter and serve immediately.

# SEARED AHI TUNA IN GINGER SOYA SESAME DRESSING

*In the global economy, "fusion" cuisine represents more than the movement between North American cooking and that of other countries. Recently, Japanese sashimi has become a popular addition to Chinese cuisine. We decided to play with that "new world" direction in this recipe.*

*Tuna, salmon, lobster and geoduck are currently favorite Chinese ingredients and this dressing works wonders on all of them. For a great finish, add a dab of wasabi, Japanese horseradish paste.*

## Dressing

| | | |
|---|---|---|
| 2 tbsp | soya sauce | 25 mL |
| 2 tbsp | *mirin* (or *sake* or sherry, sweetened with sugar to taste) | 25 mL |
| 1 tbsp | chicken stock | 15 mL |
| 2 tsp | sesame oil | 10 mL |
| 1 tbsp | grated ginger root | 15 mL |
| 2 tbsp | finely chopped green onions | 25 mL |
| | | |
| 12 oz | *ahi* tuna loin, whole piece | 375 g |
| | Salt and pepper to taste | |
| 1 tbsp | vegetable oil | 15 mL |
| 1 tbsp | toasted sesame seeds (equal parts, black and white seeds, if desired) | 15 mL |
| | Finely chopped green onions for garnish | |
| | *Wasabi* to taste (optional) | |

1. In a small bowl, combine ingredients for dressing; set aside for at least 20 minutes to blend flavors.

2. Season tuna lightly with salt and pepper.

3. Heat a heavy nonstick skillet over high heat until very hot. Add oil and heat until smoking. Add tuna and sear each side until golden, not more than 30 seconds per side. (The middle should be "blue" or very rare.)

4. To serve: Slice tuna crosswise into thin slices and arrange on a serving plate. Pour dressing evenly over fish and sprinkle with sesame seeds. Garnish with additional chopped green onions and a dab of *wasabi*, if desired.

# DRUNKEN CHICKEN WINGS

*Wine-soaked whole poached chicken, sometimes called "drunken chicken", is a popular cold dish from northern China. Our version uses chicken wings because they are inexpensive and easy to cook.*

*Chili-garlic sauce can be bought right off the shelf. Our favorite brand comes in a jar with a green lid and contains red chilies, garlic and vinegar.*

| | | |
|---|---|---|
| 8 to 10 | chicken wings | 8 to 10 |
| 2 | green onions, coarsely chopped | 2 |
| 2 tbsp | coarsely chopped ginger root | 25 mL |
| 1 tbsp | coarse salt | 15 mL |
| | Chicken stock *or* water to cover wings | |
| 3/4 cup | dry sherry *or* Chinese *shaoxing* wine | 175 mL |
| 1 tbsp | sesame oil | 15 mL |
| 2 tbsp | chopped cilantro | 25 mL |
| | Soya sauce to taste | |
| 2 tbsp | prepared chili-garlic sauce | 25 mL |

1. Cut chicken wings at the joints. Discard wing tips or reserve for making stock.

2. In a small bowl, combine green onions, ginger root and salt. Place chicken wings in a dish and spread mixture evenly over them. Set aside and allow to marinate for about 1 hour.

3. In a pot with a tight-fitting lid, combine chicken wings with enough chicken stock or water to cover. Bring to a boil and cook 1 minute. Remove from heat, cover pot and allow to steep for 10 minutes. Drain, reserving liquid. Transfer chicken to a bowl; allow to cool.

4. Add wine and 1 cup (250 mL) of reserved cooking liquid to chicken wings and mix well. Cover and refrigerate overnight. Before serving, let wings warm to room temperature; drain off liquid. Toss wings with sesame oil, cilantro, soya sauce and 1 tbsp (15 mL) chili sauce. Serve with dipping sauce on the side.

5. To make dipping sauce: In a small bowl, combine remaining chili garlic sauce with 1 tbsp (15 mL) of the wine mixture.

# CRISPY SESAME PHYLLO ROLLS STUFFED WITH GINGER CHICKEN AND SOYA ONIONS

**MAKES 16 ROLLS, SERVING 4 TO 8**

*Phyllo pastry requires a few simple techniques to make the most of its special qualities. The pastry must be handled gently and kept covered with a clean towel during use. As soon as the sheet is laid out, it must be brushed with oil. Try to work quickly with one sheet at a time. A sharp knife is helpful for cutting phyllo into manageable strips.*

**Preheat oven to 400° F (200° C)**

| | | |
|---|---|---|
| 4 | boneless skinless chicken thighs, cut into 1/4-inch (5 mm) dice | 4 |
| 1 | egg, beaten | 1 |
| 1 tbsp | minced ginger root | 15 mL |
| 1 tsp | cornstarch | 5 mL |
| | Salt and pepper to taste | |
| 1 tbsp | vegetable oil | 15 mL |
| 1 | large white onion, diced | 1 |
| 1 tsp | honey | 5 mL |
| 1 tbsp | rice vinegar | 15 mL |
| 1 tbsp | soya sauce | 15 mL |
| 1 tsp | hot sauce, such as Tabasco | 5 mL |
| 2 tbsp | vegetable oil | 25 mL |
| 1 tbsp | sesame oil | 15 mL |
| 4 | sheets store-bought phyllo pastry | 4 |
| 1 tbsp | sesame seeds | 15 mL |
| 16 | whole lettuce leaves | 16 |
| 16 | sprigs of fresh basil | 16 |

1. In a small bowl, combine chicken, egg, ginger root and cornstarch; season to taste with salt and pepper; mix well.

2. In a nonstick skillet, heat 1 tbsp (15 mL) oil over medium-high heat for 30 seconds. Add onion and honey; sauté until onion softens and begins to color, about 2 to 3 minutes. Add rice vinegar, soya sauce and hot sauce. Stir in the chicken-egg mixture; sauté for 5 minutes. The chicken should be barely cooked and the egg mixture should be set. Remove from heat and allow to cool.

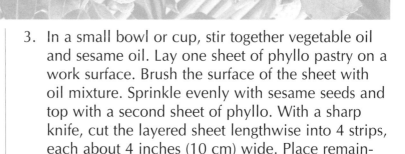

3. In a small bowl or cup, stir together vegetable oil and sesame oil. Lay one sheet of phyllo pastry on a work surface. Brush the surface of the sheet with oil mixture. Sprinkle evenly with sesame seeds and top with a second sheet of phyllo. With a sharp knife, cut the layered sheet lengthwise into 4 strips, each about 4 inches (10 cm) wide. Place remaining sheets under a kitchen towel while you make the first 8 rolls.

4. Lay the first strip of phyllo on a cutting board. With a sharp knife, cut the strip in half to make 2 shorter strips. Place 1 heaping tbsp (15 to 20 mL) of filling about 1/2 inch (1 cm) from the end of one piece. Fold this end of the pastry over the filling and squeeze into a log, then fold the sides of the phyllo over this log. Roll the log tightly until the end of the pastry strip is almost reached, then brush edge with a little sesame oil and seal. (The rolls can be made ahead to this point and refrigerated for 2 to 3 hours before cooking). Repeat procedure until all the ingredients are used up.

5. Brush the rolls with the remaining vegetable-sesame oil mixture and bake in preheated oven for 15 minutes or until golden brown and crispy. To serve: Arrange lettuce and basil on a platter. Diners assemble their own bundles by wrapping a phyllo roll in lettuce and garnishing with a leaf of basil.

# TURKEY AND SPINACH WONTONS IN CHILI-GARLIC SAUCE

*Tasty, healthy, "New World" turkey replaces pork and Chinese cabbage in this Northern Chinese favorite.*

## Filling

| | | |
|---|---|---|
| 1 | bunch spinach, washed, stems removed | 1 |
| 12 oz | ground turkey | 375 g |
| 2 | strips bacon, very finely chopped | 2 |
| 1 tbsp | cornstarch | 15 mL |
| 1 tbsp | chicken stock | 15 mL |
| 1/2 tsp | seasoned salt | 2 mL |
| | | |
| 20 to 30 | round wonton wrappers | 20 to 30 |
| 1 | egg, beaten | 1 |

## Dipping Sauce

| | | |
|---|---|---|
| 1 tbsp | minced garlic | 15 mL |
| 2 tbsp | hot bean paste | 25 mL |
| 1 tbsp | soya sauce | 15 mL |
| 2 tbsp | chicken stock | 25 mL |
| 2 tsp | sesame oil | 10 mL |
| Pinch | sugar | Pinch |

1. In a pot of boiling water, blanch spinach for about 30 seconds or until just wilted. Drain and cool immediately by plunging into a bowl of ice water. Drain. Wrap spinach in a clean towel and squeeze out as much moisture as possible. Chop finely.

2. In a mixing bowl, combine turkey with remaining filling ingredients; mix well. Fold spinach into mixture until well distributed.

3. On a work surface, lay out 4 wonton wrappers. Using a pastry brush, coat each with egg. Place 1 scant tablespoon (12 to 15 mL) of filling in the middle of each wrapper and fold to form a half moon. Press gently with fingers to squeeze out air and seal the edge, pinching it to form small pleats. Repeat with remaining ingredients, using more wrappers if required.

4. To cook wontons: Set up a steamer over high heat (see pages 18-19 for instructions) and brush rack with a bit of oil. Arrange wontons on rack, in batches, if necessary. Cover and steam until they are firm to the touch, about 5 to 7 minutes.

5. To make dipping sauce: In a small saucepan or microwaveable bowl, combine all sauce ingredients; warm until hot and fragrant (about 1 minute in microwave.)

6. Toss wontons in sauce or serve sauce on the side for dipping.

# BEEF TOMATO GARLIC SPRING ROLLS

*You can substitute pork, lamb or chicken for the beef. Just make sure to cut the meat as thinly as possible.*

*To ensure a crunchy coating on the spring roll, the oil must be very hot. A convenient way to test the temperature is to dip a wooden chopstick into the hot oil. If it bubbles rapidly, you're all set.*

| | | |
|---|---|---|
| 4 tbsp | tomato ketchup | 60 mL |
| 1 tbsp | minced garlic | 15 mL |
| 1 tbsp | *char sui* sauce *or* 2 tbsp (25 mL) barbecue sauce | 15 mL |
| 1 tbsp | rice vinegar | 15 mL |
| 1 tsp | chili sauce | 5 mL |
| 8 oz | rare roast beef, very thinly sliced | 250 g |
| 1 | medium tomato, diced | 1 |
| 1 | green onion, thinly sliced | 1 |
| 1 tsp | cornstarch | 5 mL |
| 8 | egg roll wrappers | 8 |
| 1 | medium egg, beaten | 1 |
| 1 to 2 cups | vegetable oil | 250 to 500 mL |

1. In a mixing bowl, combine ketchup, garlic, *char sui* or barbecue sauce, rice vinegar and chili sauce; mix well.

2. Place beef on a cutting board and cut into thin strips. Add to the sauce mixture along with tomato and green onion. Sprinkle with cornstarch and mix well. Set aside.

3. Lay 1 wrapper on a flat, dry work surface so it looks like a diamond-shaped square. Brush the outer edge with the beaten egg mixture. Place 2 tbsp (25 mL) of the filling in the center. Fold the corner of the wrapper closest to you over the filling, do the same with the sides, then roll into a tight cylinder. Repeat until all wrappers are filled.

4. In a small skillet, heat oil over medium-high heat until a strip of egg roll wrapper dropped into the oil immediately floats to the top. Add rolls in small batches and fry until golden brown, about 2 minutes per side. Drain on paper towel and keep warm until all rolls are cooked. Transfer to a platter and serve warm.

# PAN-FRIED POTATO, CHEDDAR AND MUSHROOM DUMPLINGS

**SERVES 4 TO 8**

*These crispy bundles make a wonderful party appetizer, especially when accompanied by GINGER GREEN ONION PESTO (see recipe, page 35) or HOISIN MAYONNAISE (instructions follow) for dipping.*

*The key to a good dumpling is ensuring that all excess air is forced from the filling before the wrapper is sealed.*

*To make HOISIN MAYONNAISE: Combine equal parts of hoisin sauce and mayonnaise.*

### Filling

| | | |
|---|---|---|
| 1 tbsp | butter | 15 mL |
| 4 oz | mushrooms, sliced | 125 g |
| 1 cup | mashed potatoes | 250 mL |
| 2 oz | grated Cheddar cheese | 50 g |
| 1 oz | grated Parmesan cheese | 25 g |
| | Salt and pepper to taste | |

### Dumplings

| | | |
|---|---|---|
| 16 | round wonton wrappers | 16 |
| 2 tbsp | water | 25 mL |
| 1 tbsp | vegetable oil | 15 mL |

1. In a nonstick skillet, heat butter over medium-high heat for 30 seconds. Add mushrooms and season with salt and pepper. Turn heat to high and sauté mushrooms until soft and most of the liquid has evaporated. Remove from heat and set aside.

2. In a small bowl, combine mashed potatoes and mushrooms. Mix well. Fold in Cheddar and Parmesan; season well with salt and pepper.

3. On a work surface, lay out 4 wonton wrappers. Using a pastry brush, coat each lightly with water. Place 1 heaping teaspoon (5 to 7 mL) of the potato mixture in the center of each round and fold to form a half moon. Press gently with fingers to squeeze out the air and seal the edges together, pinching to form small pleats.

4. In a nonstick skillet, heat oil over medium-high heat for 30 seconds. In 2 batches, cook the dumplings until golden, about 2 or 3 minutes per side, adding more oil as necessary. Drain on a paper towel. Transfer to serving plates or keep warm in oven for up to 30 minutes. Serve with dipping sauce (see suggestions, at left) or your favorite salsa.

# FIVE-SPICE POACHED BEEF

SERVES 4

*Szechuan peppercorns, which are actually dried reddish-brown berries, are available in most Chinese grocers. If you can't find them, substitute black peppercorns.*

*This beef makes a delicious appetizer served with PICKLED VEGETABLES IN HONEY RICE VINEGAR (see recipe , page 78) or YARD LONG BEAN SALAD (see recipe, page 73).*

**Cheesecloth or spice bag**

| | | |
|---|---|---|
| 1 lb | beef shank, whole cut | 500 g |

**5-Spice Mix**

| | | |
|---|---|---|
| 2 tsp | fennel seeds | 10 mL |
| 8 to 10 | whole cloves | 8 to 10 |
| 2 | star anise | 2 |
| 2 tsp | Szechuan peppercorns *or* black peppercorns | 10 mL |
| 1 | small cinnamon stick | 1 |
| 4 | slices ginger root, (about 1/4-inch [5 mm] thick) | 4 |
| 2 tbsp | soya sauce | 25 mL |
| 1 tbsp | dark soya sauce | 15 mL |
| 2 tsp | salt | 10 mL |
| 1 tbsp | sugar | 15 mL |
| 2 tbsp | white wine *or* dry sherry | 25 mL |
| 4 cups | water | 1 L |

**Dipping Sauce**

| | | |
|---|---|---|
| 1 tbsp | soya sauce | 15 mL |
| 1 tbsp | Chinese black spiced vinegar *or* balsamic vinegar | 15 mL |
| 2 tsp | sesame oil | 10 mL |
| 1 tbsp | chicken stock | 15 mL |
| 1 tbsp | chopped green onions, white part only | 15 mL |
| 1/2 tsp | dried chili flakes (optional) | 2 mL |

1. In a large pot of boiling water, boil beef shank for 1 minute. Rinse and trim off excess fat.

2. Place 5-spice mix and ginger root in a spice bag or wrap in a piece of cheesecloth and tie securely. In a heavy saucepan, combine soya sauce, salt, sugar, wine, water and spice pouch; bring to a boil. Adjust seasoning with salt and sugar.

3.  Add beef to poaching liquid. Reduce heat to simmer and cook until tender, about 1 1/2 to 2 hours. (When a chopstick inserted into the meat penetrates easily, it's cooked.) Remove from heat. Discard spice pouch; allow to cool. Refrigerate overnight.

4.  To make dipping sauce: In a small bowl, combine ingredients for sauce and mix well.

5.  To serve: Remove meat from poaching liquid; slice very thinly and arrange on platter. Serve dipping sauce on the side.

# BARBECUED PORK MUSHROOM SAUTÉ IN LETTUCE WRAP

*Soft, supple butter lettuce replaces traditional iceberg to put a new twist on this easy, tasty wrap. Store-bought barbecued pork, duck or chicken — or leftover roasts — all work well in this recipe.*

**Sauce**

| | | |
|---|---|---|
| 2 tbsp | chicken stock | 25 mL |
| 1 tbsp | oyster sauce | 15 mL |
| 1 tbsp | soya sauce | 15 mL |
| 1 tbsp | cornstarch | 15 mL |
| 4 | large dried Chinese black mushrooms | 4 |
| 6 | large dried black "cloud ear" mushrooms *or* 1 cup (250 mL) sliced bamboo shoots, cut into thin strips | 6 |
| 1 cup | boiling water | 250 mL |
| 2 tbsp | vegetable oil, divided | 25 mL |
| 3 | large eggs, beaten | 3 |
| | Seasoned salt and pepper to taste | |
| 2 tsp | minced ginger root | 10 mL |
| 1 tsp | minced garlic | 5 mL |
| 8 oz | barbecued pork, cut into strips | 250 g |
| 2 | green onions, thinly sliced | 2 |
| 2 cups | bean sprouts | 500 mL |
| | Freshly ground black pepper to taste | |
| 12 | large butter lettuce leaves | 12 |

1. In a small bowl, combine ingredients for sauce; set aside.

2. In a heatproof bowl, soak dried mushrooms in boiling water for 15 minutes or until soft. Strain and reserve liquid. Slice black mushroom into thin strips. Trim off scaly parts of cloud ear mushrooms, if using, and chop coarsely.

3. Place wok or skillet over medium-high heat until hot. Add 1 tbsp (15 mL) oil and heat for 30 seconds. Add eggs and seasoned salt and pepper to taste. Tilt and turn wok while cooking to make a thin omelet. Remove omelet and cut into thin strips, 1 inch (2.5 cm) long.

4. Add remaining oil to wok. Add mushrooms, bamboo shoots (if using), ginger root, garlic and meat; stir-fry for 1 minute. Add egg strips, green onions and sauce mixture; stir-fry for 1 minute or until most of the sauce is absorbed. (If the sauce thickens too quickly, add a little of the mushroom liquid to prevent mixture from burning.) Add bean sprouts, toss and cook briefly. Season to taste with pepper. Transfer mixture to a platter and serve with lettuce leaves on the side, so diners can make their own wraps.

# BARBECUED BACK RIBS WITH A HONEY CHILI GARLIC SAUCE

*These ribs are addictive and great for entertaining since you can make them ahead and reheat in the oven or microwave just before serving. If making ahead, don't add the sesame seeds and black pepper until ready to serve.*

*For a great main course, double the quantity.*

*If you don't have access to a barbecue, the broiler works fine.*

**Preheat broiler or start barbecue at medium-high heat**

| | | |
|---|---|---|
| 3 | slices ginger root, about 1/4 inch (5 mm) thick | 3 |
| 2 lbs | pork back ribs | 1 kg |
| 1 tbsp | vegetable oil | 15 mL |
| | Salt and pepper to taste | |
| 2 tbsp | honey | 25 mL |
| 1 tbsp | minced garlic | 15 mL |
| 1 tbsp | chili paste | 15 mL |
| 1 tbsp | dark soya sauce | 15 mL |
| 1 tbsp | rice vinegar | 15 mL |
| 1 cup | chicken stock | 250 mL |
| 1 tbsp | cornstarch dissolved in 2 tbsp (25 mL) water | 15 mL |
| | Toasted sesame seeds for garnish | |

1. Add ginger root to a large pot of boiling salted water. Add ribs and boil for 20 minutes. Drain; discard blanched ginger root. Drizzle ribs with oil and season with salt and pepper. Set aside. (This can be done up to 2 hours in advance.)

2. In a small saucepan, combine honey, garlic, chili paste, soya sauce and vinegar. Bring mixture to a boil. Remove from heat and allow flavors to infuse for at least 10 minutes.

3. On barbecue, or under the broiler, cook the ribs, turning once, until browned but still tender, about 10 to 15 minutes. Set aside to rest for 10 minutes.

4. Return sauce to heat and bring to a boil. Add chicken stock; reduce heat to simmer. Skim off any foam. Add dissolved cornstarch; stir until mixture thickens. Remove from heat.

5. On a clean work surface, cut the ribs into bite-size pieces. In a medium bowl, combine ribs and sauce and toss until well coated. Arrange on a serving platter and top with the sesame seeds and a generous sprinkling of black pepper. Serve immediately.

# SOUPS

# EGG DROP SOUP WITH MINCED BEEF AND CILANTRO

*Quick and easy with distinct flavors and a wonderful fragrance, this is a family favorite. If you don't fancy cilantro, try substituting watercress or arugula.*

| | | |
|---|---|---|
| 6 oz | lean ground beef | 175 g |
| 1/2 tsp | salt | 2 mL |
| 2 tsp | soya sauce | 10 mL |
| 1 tbsp | dry sherry *or* Chinese *shaoxing* wine | 15 mL |
| 2 tsp | minced ginger root | 10 mL |
| 3 tbsp | cornstarch, divided | 45 mL |
| 5 cups | chicken stock | 1.25 L |
| 2 | large eggs, beaten | 2 |
| 1 cup | cilantro leaves, coarsely chopped | 250 mL |
| | Salt and freshly ground white pepper to taste | |

1.  In a small bowl, combine beef, salt, soya sauce, sherry, ginger root and 1 tbsp (15 mL) of the cornstarch. Mix well and set aside to marinate for 20 minutes.

2.  In a large saucepan or soup pot, bring chicken stock to a boil. Add beef mixture, a little at a time, stirring to loosen the particles; cook for 2 minutes.

3.  Dissolve remaining cornstarch in 2 tbsp (25 mL) water; stir mixture into soup. Return to a boil, stirring until soup is slightly thickened. In a slow stream, pour eggs into soup, stirring vigorously; cook until eggs are set, about 30 seconds. Stir in cilantro. Season to taste with salt and pepper. Serve immediately.

SERVES 4

# ASPARAGUS GINGER SESAME CREAM SOUP

*This creamy, yet light, soup is bursting with the flavor of asparagus and ginger. In hot weather, it's excellent chilled.*

*For a special finish, garnish with asparagus cream. To make asparagus cream: Purée 4 spears of cooked asparagus in a food processor, then push through a strainer. Measure the purée and mix with an equal amount of sour cream. Place a spoonful of the mixture in the center of each serving and sprinkle with toasted sesame seeds.*

| | | |
|---|---|---|
| 1 tbsp | vegetable oil | 15 mL |
| 1 | large onion, coarsely chopped | 1 |
| 1 tbsp | minced ginger root | 15 mL |
| 8 oz | asparagus, trimmed and chopped | 250 g |
| 4 cups | chicken stock | 1 L |
| 1 cup | light (10%) cream | 250 mL |
| 1 tbsp | lemon juice | 15 mL |
| 1 tsp | sesame oil | 5 mL |
| | Salt and pepper to taste | |
| 2 tbsp | cornstarch dissolved in 4 tbsp (60 mL) water | 25 mL |
| | Minced fresh herbs (chives, basil thyme, rosemary, etc.), to taste | |
| 1 tbsp | toasted sesame seeds | 15 mL |

1. In a large saucepan, heat oil over medium-high heat for 30 seconds. Add onion and ginger root; cook until the onion softens and begins to change color. Add asparagus and chicken stock; bring mixture to a boil. Reduce heat and simmer for 15 minutes or until the asparagus is cooked.

2. Remove saucepan from heat and allow to cool. Transfer mixture in batches to a blender or food processor and process until smooth.

3. Pour soup through a strainer, pushing as much purée through the mesh as possible (use the back of a wooden spoon to squeeze out liquid). Return liquid to saucepan, add cream and warm to a simmer. Add lemon juice, sesame oil; season with salt and pepper. Add dissolved cornstarch; bring soup to a boil, stirring constantly until thickened. Garnish with herbs, asparagus cream (directions appear at left), if desired, and toasted sesame seeds.

# CURRIED TOMATO AND SHELLFISH BROTH

*Mustard greens, which are available in Chinese markets, give this broth an interesting bite. The combination of tomatoes and curry provides a fabulous complement to the seafood.*

| | | |
|---|---|---|
| 6 | scallops, thinly sliced | 6 |
| 8 | prawns, peeled and deveined | 8 |
| | Salt and freshly ground white pepper to taste | |
| 2 tsp | vegetable oil | 10 mL |
| 1 | small onion, sliced | 1 |
| 1 tbsp | curry powder, preferably madras | 15 mL |
| 5 cups | chicken stock | 1.25 L |
| 4 | small tomatoes, seeded and quartered | 4 |
| 12 | clams, scrubbed | 12 |
| 2 cups | thinly sliced mustard greens *or sui choy* (Napa cabbage) | 500 mL |
| | Salt and pepper to taste | |

1. Season seafood with salt and pepper; set aside.

2. In a large saucepan or soup pot, heat oil over medium heat for 30 seconds. Add onion and curry powder; sauté for 1 minute. Add chicken stock; bring to a boil. Add tomatoes and cook for 3 minutes. Add clams; cook until they open, about 2 to 5 minutes, depending on size. Skim off any impurities that rise to the top.

3. Add scallops, prawns and mustard greens or cabbage; bring to a boil. Remove from heat. Season to taste with salt and pepper. Cover and allow to steep for 2 minutes. Serve immediately.

# MIXED VEGETABLE HERB BROTH WITH SOFT TOFU

*The Asian flavor of miso, combined with traditional western herbs, enhances this savory vegetable soup.*

| | | |
|---|---|---|
| 1 tbsp | butter | 15 mL |
| 1/2 cup | diced onions | 125 mL |
| 1 cup | diced carrots | 250 mL |
| 5 cups | chicken stock *or* vegetable stock | 1.25 L |
| 3 tbsp | white or red *miso* paste | 45 mL |
| 1 cup | frozen peas | 250 mL |
| 1 cup | frozen corn kernels | 250 mL |
| 1 lb | soft tofu, cut into 1/2-inch (1 cm) cubes | 500 g |
| 2 tbsp | chopped basil | 25 mL |
| 2 tbsp | chopped parsley, preferably flat-leaf Italian variety | 25 mL |
| 1 tbsp | chopped chives | 15 mL |
| | Seasoned salt and freshly ground black pepper to taste | |

1. In a large saucepan or soup pot, melt butter over medium heat. Add onions and carrots; sauté for 1 minute. Add stock and *miso* and bring to a boil. Add peas and corn; cook for 2 minutes. Skim off any impurities that float to the top.

2. Gently stir tofu and herbs into the soup and return to a boil. Season to taste with seasoned salt and pepper. Remove from heat and serve immediately.

# BARBECUED DUCK AND MUSHROOM SOUP

*Chives are almost a vegetable component in this soup, so don't be alarmed by the quantity — an entire bunch.*

*The optional seasoning adds additional complexity to the already rich broth and is definitely worth the bit of extra effort.*

| | | |
|---|---|---|
| 4 | large dried Chinese black mushrooms | 4 |
| 1 cup | boiling water | 250 mL |
| 2 tsp | vegetable oil | 10 mL |
| 1 cup | thinly sliced button mushrooms | 250 mL |
| 1 tbsp | dry sherry *or* Chinese *shaoxing* wine | 15 mL |
| 2 cups | shredded barbecued duck meat | 500 mL |
| 5 cups | chicken stock | 1.25 L |
| 2 tsp | soya sauce | 10 mL |
| 2 tsp | dark soya sauce | 10 mL |
| 1/2 tsp | sugar | 2 mL |
| | Salt and freshly ground white pepper to taste | |
| 3 tbsp | cornstarch | 45 mL |
| 2 oz | yellow Chinese chives *or* garlic chives *or* regular chives | 50 g |
| 2 tsp | sesame oil | 10 mL |

**Optional Seasoning**

| | | |
|---|---|---|
| 1 cup | Chinese red vinegar *or* balsamic vinegar | 250 mL |
| 1 tbsp | ginger root, cut into thin julienne strips | 15 mL |
| 1 | green finger chili, thinly sliced | 1 |

1. In a heatproof bowl, soak mushrooms in boiling water for 15 minutes. Strain, reserving liquid. Discard stems and slice caps into thin strips.

2. In a large saucepan or soup pot, heat oil over medium heat. Add Chinese and button mushrooms; sauté for 2 minutes. Stir in wine. Add duck, chicken stock, soya sauces and sugar; bring soup to a boil. Reduce heat and simmer 5 minutes, skimming off any impurities that float to the top. Season to taste with salt and pepper.

3. In a small bowl, combine cornstarch and reserved mushroom liquid. Add to soup and bring to a boil, stirring to mix well. Reduce heat and simmer until the soup is slightly thickened. Stir in chives and sesame oil; remove from heat.

4. In a small heatproof bowl or pot, combine vinegar, ginger root and chili. Warm over low heat or in microwave (about 30 seconds) until heated through. Serve alongside soup, allowing diners to season according to their own taste.

# CREAMY CHINESE MUSHROOM AND POTATO SOUP

*The "wood ear fungus" called for in this recipe is often sold in Chinese markets as "tree mushroom" or "black fungus." It has been used in Chinese medicine for centuries to purify the blood and lower cholesterol. Although wood ear doesn't have much flavor, it does add a great crunchy texture. If you can't find it, button or wild mushrooms will do.*

| | | |
|---|---|---|
| 8 | dried black mushrooms (shiitake) | 8 |
| 2 | dried wood ear fungus mushrooms, *or* button or oyster mushrooms | 2 |
| 1 tbsp | butter | 15 mL |
| 1 tbsp | vegetable oil | 15 mL |
| 1 | large white onion, diced | 1 |
| 1 tbsp | minced garlic | 15 mL |
| 1 tbsp | all-purpose flour | 15 mL |
| 1 | large potato, peeled and diced | 1 |
| 6 cups | chicken stock *or* mushroom stock | 1.5 L |
| 1 tbsp | grainy mustard | 15 mL |
| | Salt and pepper to taste | |
| 4 tbsp | light sour cream | 60 mL |
| 2 tbsp | minced chives | 25 mL |

1. In a heatproof bowl or pot, soak mushrooms in 2 cups (500 mL) boiling water for 15 minutes. Drain and reserve liquid. Remove stems from dried mushrooms and cut into a fine dice. (If using fresh mushrooms, clean and finely dice.) Return dried mushrooms to reserved liquid.

2. In a large saucepan, heat butter and oil over medium-high heat for 30 seconds. Add onion and garlic; cook until the onion softens and begins to change color. Add flour and stir until absorbed into the mixture. Add potato and stock; stir well.

3. Bring mixture to a boil; reduce heat and simmer 15 minutes or until potato is cooked. Remove from heat and allow to cool. In batches, transfer to a blender or food processor and process until the mixture is smooth.

4. Return soup to saucepan; stir in mushrooms and, if necessary, thin with a little of the reserved mushroom liquid (straining out any sediment). Season with mustard, salt and pepper. Return to a boil; reduce heat and simmer 2 to 3 minutes. Serve garnished with sour cream and chives.

# Seafood and Rice Chowder

*This makes a very thick soup, not unlike a New England chowder. The corn flakes and sesame oil add a nice finishing touch.*

*Miso paste is available at Japanese grocery stores, health food stores, or sometimes at the dairy counter of supermarkets with good specialty food sections.*

| | | |
|---|---|---|
| 1 cup | short-grain rice | 250 mL |
| 2 tbsp | white *miso* paste | 25 mL |
| 8 cups | chicken stock | 2 L |
| 2 tbsp | fish sauce | 25 mL |
| 1 tbsp | dry sherry *or* Chinese *shaoxing* wine | 15 mL |
| 2 tbsp | shredded ginger root | 25 mL |
| 6 | scallops, thinly sliced | 6 |
| 8 | prawns, peeled and deveined | 8 |
| 8 oz | cod or any firm flesh white fish, thinly sliced | 250 g |
| | Salt and freshly ground white pepper to taste | |
| 2 tsp | sesame oil | 10 mL |
| 3 | green onions, finely chopped | 3 |
| 1/2 cup | corn flakes | 125 mL |

1. In a large saucepan or soup pot, combine rice, *miso* and chicken stock. Bring to a boil, watching carefully to avoid boiling over. Reduce heat to low and simmer for 1 hour or until rice grains are soft and broken up. Allow to cool slightly. In batches, transfer to a food processor or blender and process until smooth, adding more stock if soup is too thick. Return puréed soup to pot.

2. In a mixing bowl, combine fish sauce, wine and ginger root. Add seafood and fish; stir to combine. Marinate for 5 minutes.

3. Bring soup to a boil. Add seafood mixture and cook for 2 minutes. Season to taste with salt and pepper. Divide into soup bowls, drizzle with sesame oil and garnish with green onions and corn flakes. Serve immediately.

# Rice Chowder with Smoked Ham and Sweet Peas

**SERVES 4**

*Rice chowder is famous in China where it is known as congee. This hearty version is modeled on a French country soup with crunchy bread croutons for an added flourish.*

*Ham can be replaced with shredded smoked salmon or sliced grilled peppers.*

**Preheat oven to 375° F (190° C)**
**Baking sheet**

### Garlic Croutons

| | | |
|---|---|---:|
| 1 tsp | minced garlic | 5 mL |
| 2 tbsp | vegetable oil | 25 mL |
| 1 cup | bread cubes (cut to 1-inch [2.5 cm] size) | 250 mL |
| | Salt and pepper to taste | |
| 1 tbsp | grated Parmesan cheese | 15 mL |

### Soup

| | | |
|---|---|---:|
| 1 tbsp | vegetable oil | 15 mL |
| 4 oz | smoked ham, chopped | 125 g |
| 1 | large white leek, washed and chopped | 1 |
| 1 tsp | minced garlic | 5 mL |
| 2 cups | cooked rice | 500 mL |
| 6 cups | chicken stock *or* vegetable stock | 1.5 L |
| 1 cup | frozen sweet baby peas | 250 mL |
| 1 cup | chopped *sui choy* (Napa cabbage) *or* green cabbage | 250 mL |
| | Salt and pepper to taste | |

1. In a small bowl, combine garlic and oil. Spread bread cubes on baking sheet and drizzle mixture over them. Season with salt and pepper. Bake in preheated oven for 8 to 10 minutes or until lightly toasted. Remove from oven; sprinkle with Parmesan and set aside.

2. In a large saucepan, heat oil over medium-high heat for 30 seconds. Add ham, leek and garlic; cook until the leek softens and begins to change color. Add rice and chicken stock; stir to combine.

3. Bring mixture to a boil; reduce heat and simmer, stirring frequently, until the rice is split and puffed (5 to 7 minutes). Use a wooden spoon to break up the rice. (For a creamier texture, purée mixture in a food processor and return to pot.)

4. Add peas and *sui choy*; season to taste with salt and pepper. Return soup to a boil; reduce heat and simmer for 2 to 3 minutes. Serve hot, garnished with croutons.

# FRAGRANT SEAFOOD AND VEGETABLE HOT POT WITH RICE NOODLES

**SERVES 4**

*This rich seafood broth, studded with morsels of seafood and fine strands of rice noodles, is delicious and fills the kitchen with an enticing aroma.*

*Cutting the seafood into uniform chunks ensures that it will cook evenly and quickly in the hot broth.*

| | | |
|---|---|---|
| 2 oz | thin rice stick noodles *or* spaghettini | 50 g |
| 2 tsp | vegetable oil, divided | 10 mL |
| 1 | large onion, sliced | 1 |
| 1 tbsp | minced ginger root | 15 mL |
| 1 tbsp | minced garlic | 15 mL |
| 1 | lemon, juice and chopped zest | |
| 1 | red bell pepper, seeded and thinly sliced | 1 |
| 1 | carrot, peeled and thinly sliced | 1 |
| 1 cup | thinly shredded *sui choy*, (Napa cabbage) | 250 mL |
| 6 cups | fish stock *or* vegetable stock *or* clam juice | 1.5 L |
| 1 lb | assorted seafood (scallops, prawns, salmon, etc.), cut into 1-inch (2.5 cm) chunks | 500 g |
| 2 tbsp | cornstarch dissolved in 4 tbsp (60 mL) water | 25 mL |
| | Salt and pepper to taste | |
| 2 tbsp | TOASTED CHILI OIL (see recipe, page 36) | 25 mL |
| 1 tbsp | minced basil | 15 mL |

1. In a heatproof bowl or pot, soak noodles in boiling water for 5 minutes. (If using pasta, prepare according to package directions.) Drain, toss with 1 tsp (5 mL) vegetable oil and set aside.

2. In a large saucepan, heat remaining oil over medium-high heat for 30 seconds. Add onion, ginger root, garlic, lemon juice and zest. Cook until the onion softens and begins to change color. Add red pepper, carrot and cabbage; stir until well mixed.

*Recipe continues...*

RICE PAPER-WRAPPED SALMON IN HERBS WITH BALSAMIC DRESSING (PAGE 86) ➤
STIR-FRIED ASPARAGUS WITH GARLIC, SHALLOTS AND TOASTED CHILI OIL (PAGE 148)
*OVERLEAF:* YARD-LONG BEAN SALAD WITH PURPLE ONIONS IN
MUSTARD MANDARIN ORANGE DRESSING (PAGE 73)

3. Add fish stock and bring mixture to a boil; reduce heat and simmer for 15 minutes or until the vegetables are tender. Add seafood and noodles. Return to a boil; reduce heat and simmer for 2 to 3 minutes or until seafood is just cooked.

4. Add dissolved cornstarch and stir until the mixture begins to thicken. Season with salt and pepper; serve drizzled with Toasted Chili Oil and garnished with basil.

◄ Cornmeal-Crusted Snapper with Tomato Ginger Lemon Salsa (Page 83) with Pan-Fried Baby Bok Choy with Sesame Oil and Ginger (Page 146)

# RAMEN NOODLE SOUP WITH A TANGY TOMATO AND SWEET CORN BROTH

**SERVES 2 TO 4**

*This makes a quick and delicious meal.*

*If you're using stock, discard the flavor packets that usually come with ramen noodles — they're often heavily seasoned with salt and MSG and, in combination with stock, they will be overpowering.*

| | | |
|---|---|---|
| 4 cups | water *or* chicken stock | 1 L |
| 2 tbsp | tomato ketchup | 25 mL |
| 1 tbsp | *char sui* sauce *or* barbecue sauce | 15 mL |
| 1 tbsp | rice vinegar | 15 mL |
| 1 tsp | hot sauce, such as Tabasco | 5 mL |
| 1 tbsp | minced garlic | 15 mL |
| 2 | packages ramen noodles, with optional seasoning | 2 |
| 1 cup | fresh or frozen corn kernels | 250 mL |
| 1 tbsp | cornstarch, dissolved in 2 tbsp (25 mL) water | 15 mL |
| | Salt and pepper to taste | |
| 1 tbsp | minced cilantro | 15 mL |

1.  In a large saucepan, bring water or stock to a boil. Add ketchup, *char sui* or barbecue sauce, rice vinegar, hot sauce and garlic. Bring to a boil; add noodles and corn. Reduce heat to simmer and cook for 3 minutes or until noodles are soft.

2.  Add seasoning packet to taste, if using. Add dissolved cornstarch. Return to a boil; cook, stirring, until mixture thickens. Season to taste with salt and pepper. Garnish with cilantro and serve immediately.

# SALADS

SERVES 4

*This is a simple and delicious rendition of an all-time favorite. The oyster sauce stands in for traditional anchovies and complements the garlic.*

*You can easily transform this into a main course by adding slices of grilled vegetables, smoked salmon, cooked chicken, beef or seafood.*

# ASIAN CAESAR SALAD

### Dressing

| | | |
|---|---|---|
| 4 tbsp | light mayonnaise | 60 mL |
| 2 tbsp | oyster sauce | 25 mL |
| 1 tbsp | minced garlic | 15 mL |
| 1 tbsp | lemon juice | 15 mL |
| 1 tbsp | rice vinegar | 15 mL |
| 1 tbsp | chopped cilantro | 15 mL |
| | Salt and pepper to taste | |

### Salad

| | | |
|---|---|---|
| 1 | head romaine lettuce, washed | 1 |
| 1 | red or yellow bell pepper, seeded and cut into 1/2-inch (1 cm) dice | 1 |
| 1 cup | diced seedless cucumbers | 250 mL |
| 1 | green onion, thinly sliced | 1 |
| | Sesame seeds for garnish | |
| | Freshly ground black pepper to taste | |

1. In a small bowl, combine mayonnaise, oyster sauce, garlic, lemon juice, vinegar and cilantro. Season with salt and pepper; whisk until well mixed.

2. Remove root end from lettuce and wash leaves well under cold water. Tear lettuce into pieces, approximately 2 inches (5 cm) square and dry in a salad spinner or by wrapping in a clean, dry kitchen cloth. Refrigerate at least 15 minutes.

3. In a large salad bowl, combine lettuce, red or yellow bell pepper, cucumbers and green onion. Top with dressing; toss. Serve on individual salad plates with a generous sprinkling of sesame seeds and a grind of fresh pepper.

# PACIFIC RIM COLESLAW WITH SPICY APPLE-BASIL DRESSING

*A low-fat dish — it has almost no oil in the dressing — this salad is also rich in vitamins, minerals and anti-oxidants. The crunchy sunflower seeds make a perfect finish.*

## Dressing

| | | |
|---|---|---|
| 4 tbsp | rice vinegar | 60 mL |
| 4 tbsp | minced fresh basil | 60 mL |
| 2 tbsp | lemon juice | 25 mL |
| 1 tbsp | minced ginger root | 15 mL |
| 1 tbsp | minced garlic | 15 mL |
| 1 cup | unsweetened applesauce | 250 mL |
| 1 tbsp | brown sugar | 15 mL |
| 1 tsp | chili sauce | 5 mL |
| 1 tsp | sesame oil | 5 mL |
| | Salt and pepper to taste | |

## Salad

| | | |
|---|---|---|
| 1 | small head cabbage, shredded | 1 |
| 4 | carrots, shredded | 4 |
| 2 cups | bean sprouts | 500 mL |
| 1 cup | toasted sunflower seeds | 250 mL |
| 2 | green onions, thinly sliced | 2 |

1. In a small bowl, combine ingredients for dressing; mix well.

2. In a large bowl, combine ingredients for salad. Add dressing; mix well. Garnish with green onions; chill and serve.

# CHINESE-STYLE POTATO SALAD WITH FRUIT

*This Chinese version of potato salad contains fruit cocktail rather than eggs. Try using other seasonal fruits such as peaches, cherries or plums. For extra piz-zazz, arrange cooked prawns on top before serving.*

*You can buy toasted hazelnuts at a bulk food store, or toast them yourself in a frying pan. Rub skins off in a clean towel.*

### Dressing

| | | |
|---|---|---|
| 1 cup | mayonnaise | 250 mL |
| 1 tbsp | Dijon mustard | 15 mL |
| 1 tbsp | fresh lemon juice | 15 mL |
| Pinch | granulated sugar | Pinch |
| | Salt and pepper to taste | |
| | | |
| 4 cups | cubed boiled potatoes | 1 L |
| 1 cup | diced red apples | 250 mL |
| 1 cup | diced pineapple | 250 mL |
| 1 cup | seedless green grapes | 250 mL |
| 1/2 cup | toasted hazelnuts | 125 mL |
| 2 tbsp | finely chopped green onions | 25 mL |

1. In a mixing bowl, combine ingredients for dressing; mix well. Adjust seasoning with sugar, salt and pepper. Thin with a little water, if necessary.

2. In a large bowl, combine potatoes, apples and pineapples; mix well. Gently fold dressing into the mixture. Add grapes and nuts; carefully fold until well mixed. Garnish with green onions and serve.

# New Wave Beet Salad with Star Anise Dressing

*This salad is an explosion of sweet-and-sour flavor that can be made up to 2 days in advance.*

*Canned beets make an acceptable substitute, but they will lack the intensity of the roasted version.*

**Preheat oven to 375° F (190° C)**
**Roasting pan**

| | | |
|---|---|---|
| 4 | medium beets, washed | 4 |
| | Salt to taste | |
| 1 cup | vinegar (rice, wine or apple cider) | 250 mL |
| 1 tbsp | minced ginger root | 15 mL |
| 3 tbsp | honey | 45 mL |
| 1 | orange, zest and juice | 1 |
| 1 tsp | ground star anise | 5 mL |
| 2 | medium onions, peeled, halved and cut into 1/4-inch (5 mm) slices | 2 |
| | Salt and pepper to taste | |
| 1 tbsp | finely chopped cilantro | 15 mL |

1. Place beets in roasting pan and sprinkle generously with salt. Roast beets for 60 minutes or until they are easily pierced with a fork. Remove from oven and allow to cool. Trim, peel under running water and set aside.

2. In a mixing bowl, combine vinegar, ginger root, honey, orange zest, orange juice and star anise; set aside.

3. In a medium saucepan, bring 4 cups (1 L) salted water to a boil. Add onions and return to a boil; drain. Transfer onion slices to vinegar mixture.

4. Cut beets into quarters and slice each quarter into wedges approximately 1/4-inch (5 mm) wide. Add to the vinaigrette. Mix well and let the flavors infuse for at least 30 minutes. Garnish with chopped cilantro and serve chilled or at room temperature.

# Vegetable Salad with Honey Sesame Soya Vinaigrette

*This dressing can also be used on other salads, such as mesclun mix, blanched asparagus, or even simple grated carrots. For special occasions, add grilled seafood such as prawns or scallops.*

| | | |
|---|---|---|
| 2 cups | sliced blanched snow peas | 500 mL |
| 1 cup | carrots, cut into matchsticks | 250 mL |
| 1 cup | jicama, cut into matchsticks *or* sliced water chestnuts | 250 mL |

**Dressing**

| | | |
|---|---|---|
| 2 tsp | sesame oil | 10 mL |
| 2 tbsp | rice vinegar | 25 mL |
| 1 tbsp | fresh lemon juice | 15 mL |
| 2 tbsp | soya sauce | 25 mL |
| 2 tsp | honey | 10 mL |
| 1/4 cup | canola oil | 50 mL |
| 1 tsp | grated ginger root | 5 mL |
| 2 tsp | finely chopped chives | 10 mL |
| 2 tsp | toasted sesame seeds (equal parts black and white seeds, if desired) | 10 mL |
| 1 tsp | chili flakes (optional) | 5 mL |
| 1 tbsp | chopped cilantro | 15 mL |

1. In a serving bowl, combine snow peas, carrots and jicama or water chestnuts; toss to mix.

2. In a glass jar, combine ingredients for dressing; shake well. Toss with salad. Sprinkle with cilantro and serve.

# YARD-LONG BEAN SALAD WITH PURPLE ONIONS IN MUSTARD MANDARIN ORANGE DRESSING

*If fresh mandarin oranges aren't available, use the canned variety. To make mandarin orange juice: Drain and purée in a blender until liquefied.*

*Yard-long beans are available virtually year-round in Asian food markets. They look like green beans but are slender and measure a foot and a half in length. If they aren't available, green beans, yellow wax beans, sugar snap peas and asparagus all work well with this dressing.*

*For an interesting garnish, try adding CANDIED PECANS (see recipe, page 170). They will add delicious texture to the salad.*

## Dressing

| | | |
|---|---|---|
| 2 tbsp | Dijon mustard | 25 mL |
| 2 tsp | Chinese black vinegar *or* rice vinegar | 10 mL |
| 1 tsp | mandarin orange zest *or* orange zest | 5 mL |
| 1/2 cup | canola oil | 125 mL |
| 1/4 cup | mandarin orange juice (see note, at left) | 50 mL |
| 2 tsp | chopped fresh mint | 10 mL |
| Pinch | granulated sugar | Pinch |
| | Salt and pepper to taste | |
| 1 lb | yard-long beans (*or* green beans *or* a combination of green and yellow wax beans), trimmed and cut into 2-inch (5 cm) long pieces | 500 g |
| 2 | small purple onions, sliced | 2 |
| 1 tsp | finely chopped garlic | 5 mL |
| 1/2 cup | CANDIED PECANS (optional) (see recipe, page 170) | 125 mL |

1. In a mixing bowl, combine mustard, vinegar and orange zest ; mix well. Add oil in a slow stream, whisking constantly, until emulsified. Add orange juice; mix well. Fold in mint. Adjust seasoning with sugar, salt and pepper. Set aside.

2. In a large pot of salted boiling water, blanch beans until tender-crisp, about 2 minutes. (If using green or wax beans, blanch for 4 minutes or until tender-crisp.) Remove from heat; drain and cool thoroughly by plunging into ice water. Drain and pat dry with paper towels.

3. In a serving bowl, combine beans, onions, garlic and dressing; toss until vegetables are well coated. Let stand for 5 to 10 minutes. Garnish with CANDIED PECANS, if desired, and serve.

# PASTA SALAD WITH ROASTED CHICKEN AND CREAMY GINGER GREEN ONION PESTO

**SERVES 4 TO 8**

*This salad makes a nice addition to a buffet or a great lunch on its own. It also works well with penne, pasta shells or macaroni.*

*Roasted chickens are available pre-cooked at many supermarkets.*

*Vegetarians can substitute blanched asparagus or snow peas for the chicken.*

| | | |
|---|---|---|
| 8 oz | fusilli (spiral pasta) | 250 g |
| 1 cup | broccoli florets | 250 mL |
| 1/2 cup | GINGER GREEN ONION PESTO (see recipe, page 35) | 125 mL |
| 1/2 cup | light sour cream | 125 mL |
| 2 tbsp | lemon juice | 25 mL |
| 1 tbsp | honey | 15 mL |
| | Salt and pepper to taste | |
| 1 | small roasted chicken (about 3 lb [1.5 kg]), meat removed and cut into small cubes | 1 |
| 1 cup | diced cucumbers | 250 mL |
| 1 | red or yellow bell pepper, seeded and cut into 1/2-inch (1 cm) cubes | 1 |

1.  In a large pot of boiling salted water, cook pasta until *al dente*, about 8 to 10 minutes. Drain, toss with a little oil and set aside.

2.  In a large pot of boiling salted water, cook broccoli until bright green and tender, about 3 to 4 minutes. Drain, rinse under cold water and keep chilled in refrigerator until needed.

3.  In a small bowl, combine GINGER GREEN ONION PESTO, sour cream, lemon juice and honey. Season with salt and pepper; mix well.

4.  In a large bowl, combine pasta, chicken, broccoli, cucumber and pepper. Add dressing and toss well. Serve chilled.

# STICKY RICE SALAD WITH ASPARAGUS AND MUSHROOMS IN SOYA VINAIGRETTE

*"Sticky rice" is the Chinese term for any short-grained or gluti-nous rice. Italian arbo-rio or Japanese sushi rice make good substi-tutes. For this recipe, the rice must be cooked until soft, then drained and set out to dry on a baking sheet. The resulting dense, chewy rice will readily absorb the flavors of the vinaigrette.*

**Baking Sheet**

| | | |
|---|---|---|
| 2 cups | short-grained rice | 500 mL |
| 1 tsp | salt | 5 mL |
| 4 cups | water | 1 L |

**Dressing**

| | | |
|---|---|---|
| 3 tbsp | sweet soya sauce *or* SWEET SOYA SUBSTITUTE (see recipe, page 34) | 45 mL |
| 1 tbsp | mustard (yellow, Dijon or grainy) | 15 mL |
| 4 tbsp | rice vinegar | 60 mL |
| 2 tbsp | vegetable oil | 25 mL |
| 1 tsp | sesame oil | 5 mL |
| | Salt and pepper to taste | |
| | | |
| 1 tbsp | vegetable oil | 15 mL |
| 8 oz | asparagus, trimmed and cut into 1-inch (2.5 cm) pieces | 250 g |
| 1 tbsp | minced garlic | 15 mL |
| 8 oz | mushrooms, thinly sliced | 250 g |
| 1 tbsp | minced cilantro | 15 mL |

1. In a small pot, combine rice, salt and water. Bring to a boil, stir and reduce heat to low. Cover tightly and cook for 20 minutes. Remove from heat and let sit for at least 5 minutes. Spread rice evenly on a baking sheet and allow to cool to room temperature.

2. In a small bowl, combine sweet soya sauce, mustard and rice vinegar. Add the oils in a slow stream, whisking constantly. Season with salt and pepper; set aside.

3. In a nonstick skillet, heat oil over medium high heat for 30 seconds. Add asparagus, garlic and mushrooms. Sauté until asparagus is tender and mushrooms are soft, about 4 to 5 minutes.

4. In a large salad bowl, combine rice and asparagus mixture. Add dressing and toss to combine. Garnish with cilantro and serve at room temperature.

# BARBECUED GARLIC SEAFOOD SKEWERS WITH CORN AND MUSHROOM SALAD

**SERVES 2
AS A MAIN COURSE OR
4 TO 8 AS A STARTER**

*This makes a great luncheon dish for guests, an excellent starter course for a dinner party or even a one-dish dinner for two.*

*The skewers can be prepared up to 2 hours in advance and kept in the refrigerator until you're ready to grill. Brush the grill with oil just before cooking.*

*For a more dramatic effect, place the last shrimp length-wise on the skewer.*

**Preheat broiler or barbecue
Wooden skewers soaked in water for 4 hours**

### Skewers

| | | |
|---|---|---|
| 8 | shrimp | 8 |
| 4 | scallops | 4 |
| 4 oz | salmon, cut into 4 pieces | 125 g |
| 4 oz | cod, cut into 4 pieces | 125 g |
| 4 | wooden skewers | 4 |
| 1 tbsp | minced garlic | 15 mL |
| 1 tbsp | olive oil | 15 mL |
| 1 tsp | sesame oil | 5 mL |
| | Salt and pepper to taste | |

### Salad

| | | |
|---|---|---|
| 1/2 cup | light mayonnaise | 125 mL |
| 1 tbsp | rice vinegar | 15 mL |
| 1 tsp | sesame oil | 5 mL |
| 1 cup | cooked corn kernels, chilled | 250 mL |
| 2 cups | shredded lettuce | 500 mL |
| 1 cup | sliced white mushrooms | 250 mL |
| 1 cup | fresh bean spouts | 250 mL |
| | Salt and pepper to taste | |
| | Toasted sesame seeds for garnish | |

1. Thread skewers in this order: shrimp, scallop, salmon, cod, shrimp. Repeat with remaining skewers.

2. In a small bowl, combine garlic, olive oil and sesame oil. Season with salt and pepper. Coat skewers with mixture and set aside.

3. In a large bowl, combine mayonnaise, vinegar and sesame oil; mix well. Fold in the corn, lettuce, mushrooms and sprouts. Season with salt and pepper; set aside.

4. Place skewers under broiler (or on barbecue) and cook for 2 minutes per side or until the fish is just beginning to color. Serve immediately on top of the salad mixture.

# PICKLED VEGETABLES IN HONEY RICE VINEGAR

*Before a Chinese meal, a sweet-and-sour pickle of this type is often served to stimulate the appetite. Since there are no conventional courses in Chinese dining, pickled vegetables also serve the purpose of a salad, which is why we've included the recipe here. It makes a great accompaniment to FIVE-SPICE POACHED BEEF (see recipe, page 48.)*

**Pickling Liquid**

| | | |
|---|---|---|
| 2 cups | rice vinegar | 500 mL |
| 2/3 cup | honey | 150 mL |
| 1/4 tsp | salt | 1 mL |
| 2 | star anise | 2 |
| 1 | red finger chili (optional) | 1 |
| Half | small cauliflower, cut into small florets | Half |
| Quarter | small cabbage, cut into bite-sized pieces | Quarter |
| Half | long English cucumber, quartered lengthwise and cut into 1-inch (2.5 cm) pieces | Half |
| 1 | carrot, cut into 1/4-inch (5 mm) slices | 1 |

1. In a non-reactive saucepan, combine all pickling liquid ingredients except chili. Simmer over low heat until honey is melted. Add chili and set aside.

2. In a glass bowl, combine vegetables and pickling liquid. Refrigerate for 6 hours or overnight. Toss occasionally to ensure vegetables are well coated.

3. To serve: Drain pickling liquid and arrange vegetables on a serving plate.

# FISH

# STEAMED HALIBUT WITH CHINESE MUSHROOMS, HAM AND GAILAN

**SERVES 4**

For a fuller taste, use Chinese-style canned chicken stock (flavored with ginseng) and/or Chinese ham. Both are available in Chinese markets.

To make ginger juice: In a food processor or chopper, purée 8 thick slices of ginger root and 1 tbsp (15 mL) water. Extract juice by pushing pulp through a very fine sieve.

**Set up steamer
(see pages 18-19 for procedure)**

| | | |
|---|---|---|
| 6 | large dried Chinese mushrooms | 6 |
| **Marinade** | | |
| 2 tsp | fresh ginger juice (see note, at left) | 10 mL |
| 1 tbsp | fish sauce | 15 mL |
| 2 tsp | cornstarch | 10 mL |
| 1 lb | halibut fillet, cut into pieces 2 1/2 inches (6 cm) by 3/4-inch (2 cm) | 500 g |
| 4 to 6 | stems gailan, cut into bite-size lengths *or* 2 cups (500 mL) broccoli florets | 4 to 6 |
| 2 oz | prosciutto *or* Chinese ham, shaved | 50 g |
| 2 tsp | sesame oil | 10 mL |
| 2 tsp | cornstarch | 10 mL |
| 2 tbsp | chicken stock (regular or Chinese) | 25 mL |
| 1 tbsp | mushroom liquid | 15 mL |
| | Salt to taste | |

1. In a heatproof bowl or pot, soak mushrooms in 1 cup (250 mL) boiling water for 15 minutes. Strain and reserve liquid. Discard stems and slice each mushroom in half. Set aside.

2. In a mixing bowl, combine ingredients for marinade. Add fish slices and set aside to marinate for 10 minutes.

3. In a pot of boiling water, blanch gailan or broccoli for 1 minute. If using gailan, cut into bite-size lengths.

4. Arrange vegetable pieces around the edge of a serving plate which fits in steamer. Place fish pieces in the center of the plate, overlapping if necessary. Scatter mushroom pieces and ham over fish. Brush vegetables and fish with sesame oil. Place plate in steamer and steam for 5 minutes or until fish flakes easily.

5. In a small bowl, combine cornstarch, stock and mushroom liquid; stir until dissolved.

6. Remove plate from steamer. Holding a spatula against the plate to prevent contents from sliding off, pour accumulated juices into a small saucepan. Bring to a boil; add cornstarch mixture and cook over medium heat, stirring constantly, until sauce is thickened. Season to taste with salt. Pour sauce evenly over fish and vegetables and serve immediately.

# HONEY AND GARLIC SEARED HALIBUT

*The honey glaze will begin to caramelize while the fish is cooking and is a wonderful complement to the sweet, moist flavor of the halibut. This is a great dish to serve with your favorite rice and stir-fried or steamed vegetables.*

| | | |
|---|---|---|
| 2 tbsp | lemon juice | 25 mL |
| 2 tbsp | honey | 25 mL |
| 1 tbsp | olive oil | 15 mL |
| 2 tbsp | minced garlic | 25 mL |
| 1 | jalapeno pepper, seeded and minced | 1 |
| 1 1/2 lbs | fresh or frozen halibut fillets, boneless and skinless, cut into 4 equal pieces | 750 g |
| | Salt and pepper to taste | |
| 1 tbsp | vegetable oil | 15 mL |

1. In a small bowl, combine lemon juice, honey, olive oil, garlic and jalapeno pepper. Place the fish in a shallow pan and evenly coat with the mixture. Season with salt and pepper; chill in refrigerator for 5 minutes.

2. In a nonstick skillet, heat oil over medium-high heat for 45 seconds. Add the fish and sear to seal the surface and caramelize the honey, about 3 or 4 minutes per side. Reduce heat if the fish begins to char too quickly (the honey will eventually start to blacken). Serve immediately.

# Cornmeal-Crusted Snapper with Tomato Ginger Lemon Salsa

*This delicious crunchy coating seals in the flavor and works for almost any type of fish, particularly cod, halibut and trout.*

*The salsa is delicious — for extra bite, lace it with some chili sauce.*

### Salsa

| | | |
|---|---|---|
| 2 | large ripe tomatoes, diced | 2 |
| 1 tbsp | minced ginger root | 15 mL |
| 2 | green onions, thinly sliced | 2 |
| 1 | lemon, zest and juice | |
| 1 tsp | honey | 5 mL |
| | Salt and pepper to taste | |

### Fish

| | | |
|---|---|---|
| 1 cup | yellow cornmeal | 250 mL |
| 2 tbsp | Parmesan cheese | 25 mL |
| 1 lb | snapper fillets, boneless and skinless, or any firm white fish, cut into 4 equal pieces | 500 g |
| | Salt and pepper to taste | |
| 2 tbsp | vegetable oil | 25 mL |

1.  In a small bowl, combine tomatoes, ginger root, green onions, lemon zest, lemon juice and honey; mix well. Set aside.

2.  On a plate, combine cornmeal and Parmesan cheese. Season fish with salt and pepper; dredge in cornmeal mixture until well coated.

3.  In a nonstick skillet, heat oil over medium heat for 30 seconds. Add fish and fry until golden brown, about 5 minutes per side.

4.  Serve with salsa, steamed rice and Pan-Fried Baby Bok Choy with Sesame Oil and Ginger (see recipe, page 146).

# HOT POT SNAPPER WITH MUSHROOMS AND GINGER

*For a rustic touch, serve this dish in a Chinese sand pot. Fill the pot with about 1 inch (2.5 cm) hot water and place on an element over low heat until it's hot. You can also use a casserole dish filled with hot water and warmed in the microwave for 2 minutes. Drain before using.*

**9- by 13-inch (3 L) serving dish *or* Chinese sand pot**

| | | |
|---|---|---|
| 1 lb | snapper fillet, cut into 1-inch (2.5 cm) chunks | 500 g |
| 2 tsp | cornstarch | 10 mL |
| 1 | egg, beaten | 1 |
| Pinch | salt | Pinch |

**Sauce**

| | | |
|---|---|---|
| 2 tbsp | oyster sauce | 25 mL |
| 1 tbsp | soya sauce | 15 mL |
| 1 tbsp | chicken stock | 15 mL |
| 1/4 cup | vegetable oil | 50 mL |
| 1 tbsp | minced ginger root | 15 mL |
| 1 tbsp | chopped garlic | 15 mL |
| 1 | medium onion, sliced | 1 |
| 12 | large mushrooms, halved | 12 |
| 3 | green onions, cut into 2-inch (5 cm) lengths | 3 |
| | Salt and freshly ground black pepper to taste | |

1. In a mixing bowl, combine fish, cornstarch, egg and salt; marinate for 10 minutes.

2. In a small bowl, combine ingredients for glaze; stir to mix well.

3. Heat oil in wok or skillet over medium heat until just smoking. Add fish chunks separately, a few at a time, and fry until golden, about 1 minute per side. Remove with slotted spoon; drain well. Set aside, keeping fish warm.

4. Drain all but 1/2 tbsp (7 mL) oil from the wok. Increase heat to high. Add ginger root, garlic and onion; fry for 1 minute or until just beginning to color. Add mushrooms; fry for 2 minutes or until golden. Add green onions and stir-fry briefly. Add sauce mixture and bring to a boil. Add fish and fold in gently until well coated. Season to taste with salt and pepper.

5. Transfer to preheated serving dish. Serve immediately.

# RICE PAPER-WRAPPED SALMON IN HERBS WITH BALSAMIC DRESSING

*In this distinctive and delicious dish, the crisp and crunchy skin of fried rice paper seals in the moisture and the flavor of the fish. Use this technique on your favorite fish fillets, such as halibut or cod.*

| | | |
|---|---|---|
| 1 tbsp | vegetable oil | 15 mL |
| 1 tsp | TOASTED CHILI OIL (see recipe, page 35) | 5 mL |
| 1 tbsp | minced garlic | 15 mL |
| 1 tbsp | chopped chives | 15 mL |
| 1 tbsp | minced basil | 15 mL |
| 1 tbsp | minced cilantro | 15 mL |
| 1 | green onion, thinly sliced | 1 |
| | Salt and pepper to taste | |
| 4 | 8-inch (20 cm) round rice paper wrappers | 4 |
| 1 lb | salmon fillet, skin removed, cut into 4 equal pieces | 500 mL |

**Dressing**

| | | |
|---|---|---|
| 2 tbsp | balsamic vinegar | 25 mL |
| 2 tbsp | extra virgin olive oil | 25 mL |

1. In a small bowl, combine vegetable oil, chili oil, garlic, chives, basil, cilantro and green onion. Season with salt and pepper; set aside.

2. Half-fill a large heatproof bowl or pot with boiling water. Using tongs or chopsticks, immerse one sheet of rice paper at a time in water until soft and pliable, about 5 seconds. Remove and pat dry with a paper towel. Place sheet on a flat, dry surface.

3. Lay a piece of salmon in the middle of the rice paper sheet and cover with one-quarter of the herb mixture. Fold the bottom half and sides of the rice paper over the salmon, then roll into a tight bundle; set aside. Repeat until all wrappers are filled.

4. Prepare the dressing: In a small bowl, combine vinegar and olive oil. Set aside.

5. In a nonstick skillet, heat oil over medium-high heat for 30 seconds. Add bundles, season with salt and pepper and sauté until the wrapper is crisp and golden, about 3 minutes per side. Reduce heat if the wrapper browns too quickly.

6. Transfer fish bundles to a warm platter and drizzle with balsamic dressing. Serve immediately.

# PAN-FRIED SALMON SLICES WITH ORANGE AND CHAMPAGNE

*This recipe is inspired by a wonderful dish created by Chef Lam Kam Shing of Grand King Seafood Restaurant in Vancouver. Chef Lam uses only champagne in his creation, but we think the addition of orange gives it an interesting twist. Since inexpensive sparkling wine is readily available in individual-size bottles, we feel comfortable with suggesting this for a special occasion. However, white wine works equally well in the recipe.*

| | | |
|---|---|---|
| 1 lb | boneless salmon fillet, skin removed, cut into 2-inch (5 cm) by 1-inch (2.5 cm) slices | 500 g |

**Batter**

| | | |
|---|---|---|
| 2 tsp | finely chopped cilantro | 10 mL |
| 2 tsp | cornstarch | 10 mL |
| 1 | egg, beaten | 1 |
| 1/4 tsp | salt | 1 mL |
| 1/2 cup | vegetable oil | 125 mL |
| 2 tsp | minced garlic | 10 mL |
| 2 tsp | finely diced red and green chili peppers | 10 mL |
| 1/2 tsp | orange zest | 2 mL |
| 2 tbsp | fresh orange juice | 25 mL |
| 2 tbsp | champagne *or* sparkling wine *or* still white wine | 25 mL |
| | Salt to taste | |
| 1 cup | shredded iceberg lettuce | 250 mL |
| | Orange slices and sprigs of cilantro for garnish | |

1. In a bowl combine batter ingredients; mix well. Add salmon slices, coat them evenly; marinate for 15 minutes.

2. Heat oil in wok or skillet over medium heat until just smoking. Add salmon slices, a few at a time, and fry until golden, about 1 minute per side. With a slotted spoon, transfer cooked salmon to a plate lined with paper towel; keep warm until all salmon is cooked.

3. Increase heat to high. Drain all but 1/2 tbsp (7 mL) oil from the pan. Add garlic, chilies, orange zest and juice; cook, stirring, until most of the liquid is absorbed and the sauce becomes almost syrupy. Add salmon slices. Splash with champagne and toss gently until liquid is absorbed, about 30 seconds to 1 minute. Season with salt.

4. Arrange salmon attractively on a platter lined with shredded lettuce. Garnish with orange slices and cilantro. Serve immediately.

# SOLE AND ASPARAGUS ROLLS IN GINGER TOBIKKO CREAM

**Set up steamer (see pages 18-19 for procedure)**

Tobikko *is the roe of fly-ing fish, and can be found in specialty shops. If you don't want to use it, or any other roe substitute, half a can of crab meat will also yield good results — for color, add 1 tbsp (15 mL) finely diced red bell peppers with the crab.*

*Save the asparagus stems for another use.*

## Marinade

| | | |
|---|---|---|
| 1/2 tsp | salt | 2 mL |
| 1/4 tsp | white pepper | 1 mL |
| 1 | egg white, beaten | 1 |
| 2 tsp | cornstarch | 10 mL |
| 1 1/2 lbs | large boneless sole fillets, cut into 8 pieces, about 2 inches (5 cm) by 3 inches (8 cm) | 750 g |
| 8 | green onions, green parts only | 8 |
| 8 | asparagus spears, top 3 1/2 inches (8.5 cm) only | 8 |
| 1 tsp | sesame oil | 5 mL |
| 2 tsp | butter | 10 mL |
| 1 tbsp | minced ginger root | 15 mL |
| 1 tbsp | finely chopped shallots | 15 mL |
| 1 tbsp | brandy (optional) | 15 mL |
| 1/4 cup | whipping (35%) cream | 50 mL |
| 2 tsp | cornstarch, dissolved in 1/4 cup (50 mL) chicken stock | 10 mL |
| | Salt and pepper to taste | |
| 1 tbsp | *tobikko* or shrimp roe *or* red caviar | 15 mL |

1. In a bowl combine ingredients for marinade, whisking to incorporate cornstarch. Add fish and marinate for 10 minutes.

2. In a pot of boiling water, blanch green onions until just wilted and soft. Remove with slotted spoon and cool thoroughly in ice water.

3. Lay a piece of fish on work surface. Place an asparagus spear on one end; roll up and tie securely with a strand of green onion. Repeat until 8 rolls are completed.

4. Arrange rolls on a serving plate or bamboo steamer brushed with sesame oil. (See instructions for steaming, pages 18-19.) Steam for 4 minutes or until fish flakes easily. Keep warm while you make the sauce.

5. In a small saucepan, melt butter. Add ginger root and shallots; sauté for 30 seconds. Splash with brandy, if using, and cook for 30 seconds. Add cream and bring to a boil. Add dissolved corn-starch and cook until sauce is slightly thickened. Season with salt and pepper. Remove from heat and fold in *tobikko* or substitute.

6. Transfer fish to a serving plate. Pour sauce over and serve immediately.

# PAN-ROASTED TILAPIA WITH SPICY TOMATO BLACK BEAN SAUTÉ

**SERVES 4**

*Traditionally, the Chinese prefer buying fish whole and live whenever possible, as this is the ultimate standard of freshness. Unfortunately, demand and availability has driven up the prices of many wild species to the point where their use has become a luxury. Farmed tilapia is available live in Asian fish markets and is reasonably priced. If possible, buy a whole fish; otherwise, tilapia fillets or those of other firm-fleshed white fish make suitable substitutes.*

**Preheat oven to 400° F (200° C)**
**Ovenproof skillet *or* 9- by 13-inch (3 L) baking dish**

| | | |
|---|---|---|
| 1 1/2 lbs | fish fillets (tilapia, snapper or cod) | 750 g |
| 1/2 tsp | coarse salt | 2 mL |
| 1/4 tsp | freshly ground black pepper | 1 mL |
| 1/4 cup | flour | 50 mL |
| 2 tbsp | vegetable oil, divided | 25 mL |
| 2 tbsp | finely chopped onions | 25 mL |
| 2 tsp | minced ginger root | 10 mL |
| 1 tsp | finely chopped jalapeno pepper | 5 mL |
| 1 tsp | minced garlic | 5 mL |
| 2 tbsp | black bean sauce | 25 mL |
| 2 tbsp | chicken stock | 25 mL |
| 1 | large tomato, cut into 1-inch (2.5 cm) cubes | 1 |
| Pinch | granulated sugar | Pinch |
| 3 or 4 | sprigs cilantro | 3 or 4 |

1. With a sharp knife, score fish fillets in a crisscross pattern. Rub with salt and pepper. (If using a whole fish, make sure it's scaled and cleaned; score each side as above and rub with salt and pepper, inside and out.) Place flour in a plastic bag; add fish and toss until well coated.

2. Heat a heavy ovenproof skillet over high heat for 1 minute. Add 1 tbsp (15 mL) oil and heat until just smoking. Fry fish on each side until golden, about 1 minute per side. Place pan in oven (or transfer to a baking dish) and roast for 5 minutes (10 minutes if using a whole fish) or until fish flakes easily.

3. In a nonstick wok or skillet, heat remaining oil for 30 seconds. Add onions, ginger root and jalapeno; sauté for 30 seconds. Add garlic and black bean sauce; cook, stirring, another 30 seconds. Stir in chicken stock; bring to a boil. Add tomatoes; cook, stirring, for 2 minutes. Adjust flavoring with a pinch of sugar, or to taste.

4. To serve: Transfer fish to a warm platter; cover evenly with sauce and garnish with cilantro.

# Pepper and Soya Glazed Tuna with a Hong Kong-Style Butter Sauce

**Serves 4**

*Although it is no longer a British colony, Hong Kong retains considerable British influence in its cuisine — notably, in the use of sauces such as Worcestershire. The sauce for this dish is a little decadent but, combined with the richness of the tuna, it's unforgettable.*

*Steamed rice and Gailan with Balsamic Vinegar and Olive Oil (see recipe, page 150) make excellent accompaniments.*

## Sauce

| | | |
|---|---|---|
| 1 cup | white wine | 250 mL |
| 1 cup | fish stock *or* chicken stock | 250 mL |
| 1 tbsp | minced garlic | 15 mL |
| 2 tbsp | sweet soya sauce, divided *or* Sweet Soya Substitute (see recipe, page 34) | 25 mL |
| 1 lb | *ahi* or albacore tuna | 500 g |
| 1 tbsp | vegetable oil | 15 mL |
| 1 tbsp | Worcestershire sauce | 15 mL |
| | Freshly ground black pepper | |
| 2 oz | unsalted butter, chilled and cubed | 50 g |
| 2 tbsp | minced garlic chives *or* chives | 25 mL |

1. In a small saucepan over medium-high heat, combine wine, stock and garlic. Bring to a boil; cook until the liquid reduces to approximately 1/2 cup (125 mL), about 10 minutes, watching carefully to ensure the pan doesn't boil dry. Set aside.

2. On a work surface, cut tuna into slices 1 inch (2.5 cm) wide. Place slices on a plate and drizzle with 1 tbsp (15 mL) sweet soya sauce. Season with black pepper. Turn slices over to coat with sweet soya sauce.

3. In a nonstick skillet, heat oil over medium-high heat for 45 seconds. Add tuna slices and quickly sear to seal the surface and caramelize the soya sauce, about 2 to 3 minutes per side. Remove from heat and allow to rest for 2 to 3 minutes.

4. Add remaining sweet soya sauce and Worcestershire sauce to the stock mixture. Return to a simmer. Add the chunks of chilled butter, gently swirling the pan to melt the butter and build up volume in the sauce. Transfer to a warm serving dish and set aside.

5. To serve: Place tuna on a warm platter, cover with sauce and garnish with chives.

# SWEET SOYA-BRAISED COD WITH ASPARAGUS AND GARLIC

**SERVES 4**

In Chinese cooking,
cod is a treasured fish.
It's pure white, moist
and breaks into large,
succulent flakes when
perfectly cooked.
Although bones are a
problem, steaks will
greatly enhance the
flavor of this dish, but
fillets work well, if that's
your preference.

**Preheat oven to 300° F (150° C)**
**Ovenproof skillet _or_ 9- by 13-inch (3 L) baking dish**

| | | |
|---|---|---|
| 1/2 cup | flour | 125 mL |
| | Salt and pepper to taste | |
| 1 1/2 lbs | fresh or frozen cod steaks (4 steaks, approximately 1 inch [2.5 cm] thick) | 750 g |
| 2 tbsp | vegetable oil, divided | 25 mL |
| 1 tbsp | sliced garlic | 15 mL |
| 1 tbsp | minced ginger root | 15 mL |
| 1 tsp | chili sauce | 5 mL |
| 8 oz | asparagus, trimmed and cut into 2-inch (5 cm) pieces | 250 g |
| 2 cups | fish stock | 500 mL |
| 2 tbsp | sweet soya sauce or SWEET SOYA SUBSTITUTE (see recipe, page 34) | 25 mL |
| 1 tsp | sesame oil | 5 mL |
| 1 tbsp | cornstarch dissolved in 2 tbsp (25 mL) water | 15 mL |

1. On a plate, combine flour, salt and pepper. Dredge fish in mixture until evenly coated.

2. In a large ovenproof skillet, heat 1 tbsp (15 mL) oil over medium-high heat for 30 seconds. Add fish and fry until golden brown, about 3 minutes per side. Transfer to a warm plate.

3. Return the pan to stove and heat 1 tbsp (15 mL) oil for 30 seconds. Add garlic, ginger root, chili sauce and asparagus. Stir well and heat for 1 minute. Add fish stock, sweet soya sauce and sesame oil; bring to a boil. Add dissolved cornstarch and stir until the mixture thickens. Return cod to the pan or transfer to baking dish. Cook in preheated oven for 5 minutes. Serve immediately with steamed rice and vegetables.

CRISP-FRIED CHILI AND GARLIC SHRIMP (PAGE 98) ➤

_OVERLEAF:_ STIR-FRIED CLAMS WITH ORANGE AND BLACK BEAN SAUCE (PAGE 103)

# SEAFOOD

◄ PAN-FRIED PORK CHOPS WITH SUN-DRIED TOMATOES AND CILANTRO (PAGE 138)

# CRISP-FRIED CHILI AND GARLIC SHRIMP

*The shells on the shrimp in this savory dish should be crispy. The best way to eat them is whole, shells and all. If that makes you uneasy, peel them when they're served although you'll lose some flavor.*

| | | |
|---|---|---|
| 1 lb | medium tiger prawns or large shrimp, unshelled, heads removed, cleaned and deveined | 500 g |
| 1 cup | cornstarch | 250 mL |
| 1/2 tsp | salt | 2 mL |
| 1/4 tsp | freshly ground black pepper | 1 mL |
| 2 cups + 1 tbsp | vegetable oil | 500 mL + 15 mL |
| 1 tbsp | finely chopped garlic | 15 mL |
| 1 tsp | dried chili flakes | 5 mL |
| 1/4 cup | finely chopped green peppers | 50 mL |
| 1 tbsp | dry sherry *or* Chinese *shaoxing* wine | 15 mL |
| 1 tbsp | soya sauce | 15 mL |

1. Wash shrimp or prawns thoroughly and soak in cold salted water for 15 minutes. Pat dry with paper towels.

2. In a plastic bag, combine cornstarch, salt and pepper. Add shrimp and toss until well coated.

3. In a wok, heat oil over medium-high heat until just smoking. Shake excess coating off shrimp and fry, a handful at a time, until crisp and golden, about 1 minute per side. Spoon hot oil over shrimp from time to time to facilitate cooking. With a slotted spoon, transfer cooked shrimp to a plate lined with paper towel; keep warm until all are cooked.

4. Drain oil from wok; wipe clean and add 1 tbsp (15 mL) oil to the pan. Add garlic, chili and peppers; stir-fry until fragrant, about 30 seconds. Increase heat to high. Add shrimp; toss to mix for 30 seconds. Splash with sherry and soya sauce; toss vigorously until liquid is completely absorbed. Transfer to a platter and serve immediately.

# Sautéed Shrimp and Mixed Peppers in Maple and Mustard Glaze

**Serves 4**

*While it's cooking, the shrimp fills the kitchen with intoxicating aromas of mustard, chilies and maple. Quick and elegant, this dish is ideal for entertaining since everything can be done ahead except for the brief cooking.*

*Steamed rice and vegetables make ideal accompaniments.*

| 1 tbsp | vegetable oil | 15 mL |
| 1 | large onion, sliced | 1 |
| 1 | red bell pepper, seeded and finely diced | 1 |
| 1 | yellow pepper, seeded and finely diced | 1 |
| 1 | green pepper, seeded and finely diced | 1 |
| 1 lb | shrimp, shelled and deveined | 500 g |
| 1 tsp | TOASTED CHILI OIL (see recipe, page 36) | 5 mL |
| 2 tbsp | grainy mustard | 25 mL |
| 1 tbsp | rice vinegar | 15 mL |
| 1 tbsp | maple syrup | 15 mL |
| 1 tbsp | minced cilantro | 15 mL |
| | Salt and pepper to taste | |

1. In a nonstick wok or skillet, heat oil over medium heat for 30 seconds. Add onion and peppers; cook until the peppers begin to soften and the color brightens, about 2 to 3 minutes.

2. Add the shrimp and cook until they turn pink and opaque. Add chili oil, mustard, rice vinegar, maple syrup and cilantro. Stir well and cook an additional 2 minutes. Season to taste, transfer to a platter and serve immediately.

# BEER-BATTERED SHRIMP WITH HONEY-CHILI GLAZE

This dish showcases the Chinese technique of coating deep-fried dishes with a sweet-and-sour sauce. Honey, ginger, rice vinegar and chilies give a tangy sweetness to this version of the classic sauce.

## Batter

| | | |
|---|---|---|
| 1/2 cup | beer | 125 mL |
| 1 cup | cold water | 250 mL |
| 1 cup | flour | 250 mL |
| 1 tsp | baking powder | 5 mL |
| 1/2 cup | cornstarch | 125 mL |
| 1 tsp | salt | 5 mL |
| 1 tsp | freshly ground black pepper | 5 mL |
| 2 | egg yolks, beaten | 2 |

## Glaze

| | | |
|---|---|---|
| 2 tbsp | honey | 25 mL |
| 2 tbsp | rice vinegar | 25 mL |
| 1 tbsp | minced ginger root | 15 mL |
| 1 tsp | chili paste | 5 mL |
| 1 tsp | sesame oil | 5 mL |

## Shrimp

| | | |
|---|---|---|
| 4 cups | vegetable oil | 1 L |
| 1 lb | shrimp, shelled and deveined | 500 g |
| 1/4 cup | cornstarch | 50 mL |
| 2 cups | shredded head lettuce | 500 mL |

1. In a small bowl, combine beer, water, flour, baking powder, cornstarch, salt, pepper and egg yolks. Mix well and set aside for at least 15 minutes.

2. In a small bowl, combine honey, rice vinegar, ginger root, chili paste and sesame oil. Set aside.

3. In a heavy-bottom pot or deep fryer, heat oil to 275° F (140° C) or until a spoonful of batter dropped in the oil bubbles rapidly to the top. In a plastic bag, toss shrimp with cornstarch until evenly coated. Stir reserved batter, then dip shrimp in the mixture to coat well. Fry in hot oil, 6 at a time, until golden and crisp, 2 to 3 minutes per side. Transfer cooked shrimp to a paper towel-lined plate and keep warm until all are cooked.

4. In a mixing bowl, toss cooked shrimp with the glaze. Place finely shredded lettuce on a serving plate and top with the glazed shrimp. Serve immediately.

# STEAMED SHRIMP-STUFFED TOFU WITH BROCCOLI

**SERVES 4**

*This is one of our favorite adaptations from classical Cantonese cooking. If you've been telling yourself to eat more tofu for its health benefits, this should convince you that it can also be delicious.*

**Preheat steamer over medium-high heat
(see procedure, pages 18-19)**

## Stuffing

| | | |
|---|---|---|
| 8 oz | raw shrimp, coarsely chopped | 250 g |
| 1 tsp | minced ginger root | 5 mL |
| 1/2 cup | water chestnuts, finely chopped | 125 mL |
| 2 tbsp | finely chopped green onions | 25 mL |
| 1 | egg white, beaten | 1 |
| 1/4 tsp | salt | 1 mL |
| 1 tbsp | cornstarch | 15 mL |
| 1 lb | soft tofu | 500 g |
| 2 cups | broccoli florets, cut into bite-sized pieces | 500 mL |

## Sauce:

| | | |
|---|---|---|
| 2 tsp | sesame oil | 10 mL |
| 2 tbsp | soya sauce | 25 mL |
| 1 tbsp | chicken stock | 15 mL |
| Pinch | granulated sugar | Pinch |

1. In a mixing bowl, combine ingredients for stuffing; mix well and set aside.

2. Drain liquid from tofu package. Gently cut tofu in half lengthwise, then slice each half into 1/2-inch (1 cm) thick slices. Gently pat pieces dry with paper towel. Lay tofu pieces in a flat layer in the center of a plate that will fit into steamer. Line the outside of the plate with a ring of broccoli florets. Spoon a portion (about 1 tbsp [15 mL]) of shrimp stuffing onto each slice of tofu, pressing gently with the back of the spoon so it sticks to the tofu.

3. Place the plate in preheated steamer, cover and steam for 5 minutes or until shrimp mixture is firm to the touch.

4. In a small saucepan, heat ingredients for sauce until just boiling. When shrimp is cooked, pour sauce evenly over tofu and broccoli and serve immediately.

# STIR-FRIED CLAMS WITH ORANGE AND BLACK BEAN SAUCE

**SERVES 4**

*Orange juice adds a nice tang to this all-time classic favorite.*

| | | |
|---|---|---|
| 2 lbs | fresh clams | 1 kg |
| 1 tbsp | vegetable oil | 15 mL |
| 2 tbsp | chopped onions | 25 mL |
| 2 tsp | minced garlic | 10 mL |
| 2 tsp | minced ginger root | 10 mL |
| 2 tbsp | black bean sauce | 25 mL |
| 1 tbsp | dry sherry *or* Chinese *shaoxing* wine | 15 mL |
| 1 tbsp | oyster sauce | 15 mL |
| 2 tbsp | frozen orange juice concentrate, thawed | 25 mL |
| 1/2 cup | diced green peppers | 125 mL |
| 1/2 cup | diced red bell peppers | 125 mL |

1. Wash and scrub clams well by rubbing them together under cold running water. Drain and set aside.

2. Heat oil in wok or heavy saucepan over medium-high heat until just smoking. Add onions, garlic, ginger root and black bean sauce; stir fry until fragrant, about 1 minute.

3. Add clams, sherry, oyster sauce and orange juice concentrate; stir to mix. Cover and steam for 5 minutes or until clams open. Shake the wok or saucepan occasionally to facilitate this process. Discard any clams that fail to open.

4. Uncover the pan, increase heat to high and add peppers. Stir-fry for about 1 minute until peppers are warmed through and sauce is reduced slightly. Transfer to serving dish and serve immediately.

# CRAB AND GREEN ONION CAKES WITH GINGER-SESAME AÏOLI

*The fish base for these cakes adds richness and moisture. For a very special taste, substitute scallops or shrimp for the fish.*

### Ginger Sesame Aïoli

| | | |
|---|---|---|
| 5 tbsp | mayonnaise | 75 mL |
| 5 tbsp | GINGER GREEN ONION PESTO (see recipe, page 35) | 75 mL |

### Cakes

| | | |
|---|---|---|
| 1 cup | bread cubes | 250 mL |
| | Hot water | |
| 8 oz | sole or snapper filets, deboned | 250 g |
| 2 | egg whites | 2 |
| 2 tbsp | ginger-sesame aïoli | 25 mL |
| 8 oz | crab meat, fresh or canned | 250 g |
| 4 | green onions, sliced | 4 |
| | Salt and pepper to taste | |
| 1/3 cup | flour | 75 mL |
| 1 tbsp | butter | 15 mL |
| 1 tbsp | vegetable oil | 15 mL |

1. In a small bowl, combine mayonnaise and pesto to make aïoli. Set aside.

2. In a small bowl, combine bread and enough hot water to cover; let sit for 10 minutes. Pour off excess water and gently squeeze the bread to remove most of the moisture.

3. In a food processor, combine fish, moist bread, egg whites and 2 tbsp (25 mL) of the aïoli. Process until the mixture is a smooth paste, about 1 minute. Place mixture in a medium-sized bowl. Add crab and green onions; season with salt and pepper. Fold until combined.

4. Make the cakes: With your hands, form approximately 1/4 cup (50 mL) of the mixture into a ball then flatten gently into a patty. Spread flour on a plate; dredge patty with flour to coat both sides. Repeat until all the mixture is used (you should have 8 patties).

5. In a nonstick skillet, heat butter and oil over medium-high heat for 30 seconds. Add crab cakes and cook until crisp and golden, about 5 minutes per side. Serve with aïoli on the side.

# CRAB IN GINGER COCONUT CREAM WITH CHIVES

**SERVES 2 TO 4**

*This treatment of crab is delicious and very popular in Chinese restaurants in North America.*

*If you don't have coconut milk, half and half (10%) or heavy (35%) cream will do.*

*Always purchase crab live from your seafood supplier and have them clean it for you. To choose the best crabs, pinch the back legs; if they are firm, the crab will be meaty; if not, pick another.*

*If you're in the mood to splurge, make this with a large lobster. The serving size reflects our assumption that this would be served as part of a Chinese meal, with other dishes.*

| | | |
|---|---|---|
| 1 | large whole crab, about 2 to 3 lbs (1 to 1.5 kg), cleaned; *or* 2 smaller crabs, back shell removed and set aside | 1 |
| 1 cup | flour | 250 mL |
| 1/2 tsp | salt | 2 mL |
| 1/4 tsp | freshly ground black pepper | 1 mL |
| 2 cups | vegetable oil | 500 mL |
| 6 | slices ginger root | 6 |
| 2 tbsp | chopped onions | 25 mL |
| 1 cup | coconut milk | 250 mL |
| 1/2 cup | milk | 125 mL |
| | Salt and pepper to taste | |
| 1 tbsp | cornstarch dissolved in 1/2 cup (125 mL) chicken stock | 15 mL |
| 2 tbsp | chopped chives *or* green onions | 25 mL |

1. Using a heavy knife, cut the crab across the body, with legs attached, into 8 pieces. Pat pieces dry with paper towels. In a plastic bag, combine flour, salt and pepper. Add crab and toss until well coated.

2. Heat oil in a wok over medium-high heat until just smoking. Add crab, after shaking off excess flour, a few pieces at a time; fry until golden, about 2 minutes per side. Spoon hot oil over the crab from time to time to facilitate cooking. Remove; drain on paper towel and keep warm. If you want to use the shell for decoration, fry it as well.

3. Drain all but 1 tbsp (15 mL) oil from the wok. Add ginger root and onions; stir-fry until fragrant, about 1 minute. If you want to use the roe — it's the yellow creamy paste under the shell of female crabs and it will greatly improve the taste of the sauce — strain it through a fine sieve and stir-fry with the vegetables. Add coconut milk and milk; mix well and bring to a boil.

4. Return crab to the pan and cook 1 minute. Season to taste with salt and pepper. Add dissolved cornstarch and stir until sauce is thickened. Add chives and stir to mix well; arrange crab pieces on serving platter; garnish with shell, if using, and serve immediately.

# CRAB, BOK CHOY AND CHEDDAR EGG FOO YUNG

**SERVES 4**

*This is a great dish for a special brunch or when you're entertaining house guests.*

*If using canned crab, check its salt content (some canned crab is high in sodium) and adjust the seasoning according to taste.*

*You can speed the cooking by switching your oven to broiler after 3 to 4 minutes. Watch carefully and remove once the cheese starts to bubble.*

**Preheat oven to 350° F (180° C)**
**Ovenproof skillet**

| | | |
|---|---|---|
| 6 | large eggs | 6 |
| 1 cup | milk | 250 mL |
| 2 | green onions, finely sliced | 2 |
| 4 oz | crab meat | 125 g |
| 1 cup | finely chopped bok choy | 250 mL |
| | Salt and pepper to taste | |
| 1 tbsp | vegetable oil | 15 mL |
| 1 cup | shredded Cheddar cheese | 250 mL |
| 1 tsp | sesame oil | 5 mL |

1. In a medium bowl, whisk eggs and milk together until well blended. Add onions, crab and bok choy. Season with salt and pepper; stir to combine.

2. In an ovenproof skillet, heat oil over medium heat for 30 seconds. Add egg mixture and stir with a spatula until the egg begins to scramble but is still fairly moist. Spread Cheddar over top and bake for 7 to 8 minutes or until the egg is firmly set and the cheese is melted. Remove from oven; drizzle with sesame oil and serve straight from pan.

# BREADED SCALLOP SKEWERS WITH BLACK BEAN SAUCE

**4 wood skewers**

## Scallops

| | | |
|---|---|---|
| 16 | large scallops | 16 |
| 1 | egg | 1 |
| 2 tbsp | milk | 25 mL |
| | Salt and pepper to taste | |
| 1/2 cup | all-purpose flour | 125 mL |
| 1 cup | fresh bread crumbs | 250 mL |

## Black Bean Sauce

| | | |
|---|---|---|
| 1 cup | chicken stock | 250 mL |
| 2 tbsp | black bean sauce | 25 mL |
| 1 tbsp | minced ginger root | 15 mL |
| 1 tbsp | cornstarch dissolved in 2 tbsp (25 mL) water | 15 mL |
| 1 tbsp | butter | 15 mL |
| 1 tbsp | vegetable oil | 15 mL |

1. Thread 4 scallops onto each skewer.

2. In a shallow dish, whisk together egg and milk. Season scallops with salt and pepper, roll in flour, then in egg mixture and, finally, in bread crumbs, ensuring that the scallops are well-covered. Shake off excess crumbs and set aside.

3. In a small saucepan, combine chicken stock, black bean sauce and ginger root. Bring to a boil, add dissolved cornstarch and stir until the mixture begins to thicken. Set aside until scallops are ready.

4. In a nonstick pan, heat butter and oil over high heat until the butter begins to foam. Add skewers and reduce heat to medium-high. Cook until scallops are golden brown, about 3 minutes per side. To serve: Pour warm sauce on a plate and lay the skewers on top. Serve immediately.

**SERVES 4**

*In this simple treatment, a coating of freshly-made bread crumbs seals in the juices of the scallops. The results are both elegant and succulent.*

*Although store-bought crumbs are an acceptable alternative, it's worth the bit of extra effort to make your own. To make bread crumbs: Cut off crusts and cube; pulse in a food processor until you have the desired results.*

*The scallops are great served with steamed rice and vegetables.*

# ASIAN SEAFOOD AND TOMATO STEW

**SERVES 4**

*In this recipe, the classic combination of tomato and garlic is enlivened with horseradish and toasted chili oil. The seafood is lightly poached in the hot broth and will cook very quickly.*

*This is great over steamed rice.*

**Preheat oven to 350° F (180° C)**

| | | |
|---|---|---|
| 4 cups | tomato juice | 1 L |
| 2 cups | chicken stock | 500 mL |
| 1 tbsp | minced garlic | 15 mL |
| 1 tbsp | minced ginger root | 15 mL |
| 2 tbsp | honey | 25 mL |
| 1 | medium onion, thinly sliced | 1 |
| 2 tbsp | horseradish | 25 mL |
| 1 | red bell pepper, seeded and finely diced | 1 |
| 12 oz | seafood (shrimp, peeled and deveined, and/or scallops) | 375 g |
| 1 lb | mussels and/or clams | 500 g |
| 1 cup | shredded bok choy | 250 mL |
| 2 tbsp | cornstarch dissolved in 4 tbsp (60 mL) water | 25 mL |
| 1 tbsp | minced cilantro | 15 mL |
| 1 tbsp | TOASTED CHILI OIL (see recipe, page 35) | 15 mL |
| | Salt and pepper to taste | |

1. In a medium saucepan, combine tomato juice, chicken stock, garlic, ginger root, honey, onion, horseradish and red bell pepper. Bring to a boil. Reduce heat and simmer for 20 minutes.

2. Add seafood, mussels or clams and bok choy; simmer until seafood is tender and all shells have opened (discard those that fail to open after 5 minutes). Add dissolved cornstarch; stir until mixture thickens. Season with cilantro, chili oil, salt and pepper. Serve immediately.

# POULTRY

# ROCK SALT PAN-ROASTED CHICKEN IN GARLIC SESAME AND OLIVE OIL

*Perhaps because chicken was first domesticated in China and later exported to all corners of the world, the Chinese have a special affinity for dishes featuring crispy roasted poultry. In this recipe, seasoning the bird with coarse salt and roasting to a golden brown brings out the flavor of the chicken and produces a delicious crispy skin. Simple and elegant, hot or cold, this is true comfort food.*

**Preheat oven to 375° F (190° C)**

**10-inch (25 cm) ovenproof frying pan or cast iron skillet *or* 9- by 13-inch (3 L) baking dish**

| | | |
|---|---|---|
| 2 tbsp | olive oil | 25 mL |
| 1 | onion, thinly sliced | 1 |
| 1 | head garlic, separated into cloves, peeled | 1 |
| 3 lbs | chicken pieces | 1.5 Kg |
| 2 tbsp | coarse salt (sea salt or pickling salt) | 25 mL |
| 1 tsp | sesame oil | 5 mL |
| | Cracked black pepper to taste | |
| | GINGER GREEN ONION PESTO, *optional* (see recipe, page 35) | |

1. In a skillet, preferably ovenproof, heat oil over high heat for 30 seconds. Add onions and garlic; sauté 2 minutes. (If you don't have an ovenproof skillet, transfer sautéed garlic and onions to baking dish and proceed as follows.)

2. Arrange chicken pieces on top of onion mixture; sprinkle evenly with salt and drizzle with sesame oil. Place the skillet or baking dish in preheated oven and roast for 45 minutes or until the skin is golden brown. Remove from oven; allow to rest 2 to 3 minutes.

3. Transfer to a platter and serve with steamed rice and GINGER GREEN ONION PESTO, if desired.

# FOIL-WRAPPED CHICKEN BUNDLES WITH GREEN ONION AND BLACK BEAN SAUCE

**Preheat oven to 375° F (190° C)**

*These tasty bundles are simple to make and wonderful to eat. The tinfoil container roasts and steams the chicken simultaneously. The results are delicious — and addictive.*

| | | |
|---|---|---|
| 4 tbsp | black bean sauce | 60 mL |
| 1 tsp | chili oil | 5 mL |
| 1 tsp | sesame oil | 5 mL |
| 6 | green onions, cut into 1-inch (2.5 cm) pieces | 6 |
| 8 to 10 | thin slices ginger root | 8 to 10 |
| 3 lbs | chicken pieces | 1.5 kg |
| | Cracked black pepper | |

1.  In a large bowl, combine bean sauce, chili and sesame oil, green onions and ginger root. Add chicken and toss to mix well.

2.  Lay out a 12-inch (30 cm) strip of tinfoil on a work surface. Place 2 pieces of chicken on the foil and season with pepper. Fold the ends of the tinfoil over top the chicken and fold in the sides to make a tight seal. Repeat procedure for remaining pieces of chicken.

3.  Bake bundles in a preheated oven for 30 minutes. Remove from oven and allow to rest 10 minutes. Serve individual packages with grilled or sautéed vegetables and steamed rice.

# SHREDDED CHICKEN AND CHINESE CABBAGE IN SPICY TOMATO SAUCE

*This recipe makes a quick and nutritious meal that can be ready in 20 minutes. Feel free to substitute your favorite vegetables for the sui choy; broccoli, spinach, green cabbage and snow peas are all good choices.*

| | | |
|---|---|---|
| 8 oz | chicken breast, thinly sliced | 250 g |
| 3 tbsp | cornstarch, divided | 45 mL |
| 1 tbsp | vegetable oil | 15 mL |
| 2 cups | tomato juice | 500 mL |
| 1 cup | chicken stock | 250 mL |
| 1 tbsp | minced garlic | 15 mL |
| 1 tsp | chili paste | 5 mL |
| 1 tbsp | sweet soya sauce *or* SWEET SOYA SUBSTITUTE (see recipe page 34) | 15 mL |
| 2 cups | shredded *sui choy* (Napa cabbage) | 500 mL |
| 1 tbsp | fresh basil, finely chopped | 15 mL |
| 4 | green onions, cut into 1/2-inch (1 cm) slices | 4 |
| | Salt and pepper to taste | |

1. In a bowl combine chicken and 2 tbsp (25 mL) cornstarch; mix well. Set aside.

2. In a small bowl, mix remaining 1 tbsp (15 mL) cornstarch with 2 tbsp (25 mL) water. Stir until dissolved.

3. In a nonstick wok or skillet, heat oil over high heat for 30 seconds. Add chicken and sauté until it begins to brown and is no longer pink. Transfer to a plate.

4. Return pan to stove. Add tomato juice, chicken stock, garlic, chili paste, and sweet soya sauce; bring to a boil. Add dissolved cornstarch; stir until the mixture begins to thicken.

5. Add *sui choy*, basil and green onions; stir until heated through, about 1 or 2 minutes. Return chicken and juices to the pan and heat for an additional 1 to 2 minutes. Season with salt and pepper. Serve immediately over steamed rice.

POULTRY **115**

# BARBECUED CHICKEN BREAST WITH LEMON GINGER SAUCE

**Preheat broiler or start barbecue**

**SERVES 4**

*In this recipe, GINGER GREEN ONION PESTO chars the surface of the chicken and infuses it with flavor. This recipe, which also works well with chicken legs and thighs, is great with steamed rice and your favorite vegetables.*

| | | |
|---|---|---|
| 4 | boneless chicken breasts | 4 |
| 1/2 cup | GINGER-GREEN ONION PESTO (see recipe, page 35) | 125 mL |
| | Salt and pepper to taste | |

**Lemon Ginger Sauce**

| | | |
|---|---|---|
| 1 | lemon, zest and juice | 1 |
| 2 tbsp | honey | 25 mL |
| 1 tsp | TOASTED CHILI OIL (see recipe, page 36) | 5 mL |
| 1 tbsp | minced ginger root | 15 mL |
| 1 cup | chicken stock | 250 mL |
| 2 tbsp | cornstarch, dissolved in 4 tbsp (60 mL) water | 25 mL |

1. Coat chicken with pesto mixture; season with salt and pepper. Set aside to marinate for 10 minutes.

2. Grill or broil chicken, skin-side first, until cooked through, about 6 or 7 minutes per side. Transfer to a platter and keep warm.

3. In a small saucepan, combine lemon zest and juice, honey, chili oil, ginger root, and chicken stock; mix well. Bring to a boil. Add dissolved cornstarch; stir until sauce thickens.

4. To serve: Slice chicken thinly and top with the lemon ginger sauce.

# STIR-FRIED CHICKEN WITH PEACHES AND PICKLED GINGER

*In this recipe, the sweetness of the peaches strikes a wonderful balance with the peppery bean paste and the slightly tart pickled ginger. Although canned peaches work very well, feel free to use fresh peaches in season.*

*Peel peaches as you would a tomato by dipping them in boiling water for about 30 seconds.*

## Marinade

| | | |
|---|---|---|
| 2 tbsp | soya sauce | 25 mL |
| 1/4 tsp | salt | 1 mL |
| Pinch | white pepper | Pinch |
| 2 tsp | cornstarch | 10 mL |
| 12 oz | boneless, skinless chicken breast, thinly sliced | 375 g |

## Sauce

| | | |
|---|---|---|
| 2 tbsp | pickled ginger liquid | 25 mL |
| 1 tbsp | ketchup | 15 mL |
| 1 tsp | hot bean paste | 5 mL |
| 2 tbsp | chicken stock | 25 mL |
| 1 tbsp | vegetable oil | 15 mL |
| 1/2 cup | roasted cashews | 125 mL |
| 12 | slices pickled ginger, cut into thin strips | 12 |
| 1 tsp | minced garlic | 5 mL |
| 2 | stalks celery, cut diagonally into thin strips | 2 |
| 1 1/2 cups | sliced canned peaches | 375 mL |
| | Salt, pepper and sugar to taste | |

1. In a bowl combine ingredients for marinade. Add chicken; mix well. Marinate for 30 minutes.

2. In a small bowl, combine ingredients for sauce; set aside.

3. In a wok or nonstick skillet, heat oil over medium-high heat for 30 seconds. Add cashews and fry until golden brown and crispy, about 1 minute. Remove with slotted spoon and set aside.

4. In the same pan, fry ginger and garlic until fragrant, about 30 seconds. Add chicken; stir-fry 2 minutes. Add celery; stir-fry for 1 minute. Add sauce mixture along with peaches; stir to mix until sauce is slightly thickened. Season to taste with salt, pepper and sugar, if desired. Add cashews and toss to mix. Transfer to serving platter and serve immediately.

# CHILI SOYA ROASTED CHICKEN

**SERVES 4**

*Inspired by the poached soya chicken available in Chinese barbecue shops, this roasted version has a delicious smoky, spicy-sweet flavor.*

**Preheat oven to 425° F (220° C)**

| | | |
|---|---|---|
| 1 | roasting chicken (2 to 3 lbs [1 to 1.5 kg]) | 1 |
| 1 tbsp | garlic salt | 15 mL |
| 1 tsp | 5-spice powder | 5 mL |
| 3 | slices ginger root | 3 |
| 2 | green onions, smashed with the flat side of a knife | 2 |

**Basting Sauce**

| | | |
|---|---|---|
| 1 tbsp | dark soya sauce | 15 mL |
| 1 tbsp | soya sauce | 15 mL |
| 1 tbsp | chili sauce | 15 mL |
| 1 tbsp | honey | 15 mL |

1. Wash chicken well and pat dry with paper towels.

2. In a small bowl, combine garlic salt and 5-spice powder. Rub chicken with mixture, inside and out. Place ginger and green onions in cavity. Truss chicken with string.

3. In a small bowl, combine ingredients for basting sauce; mix well. Set aside.

4. Roast chicken at 425° F (220° C) for 15 minutes. Reduce heat to 375° F (190° C) and continue roasting until the thigh has an internal temperature of 160° F (70° C), about 1 to 1 1/4 hours. During the last 30 minutes, baste chicken frequently with basting sauce. When chicken is cooked, remove from oven and allow to rest for 5 to 10 minutes. Cut into bite-size pieces, arrange on platter and serve immediately.

# BARBECUED CHICKEN WITH MUSTARD ORANGE AND HOISIN GLAZE

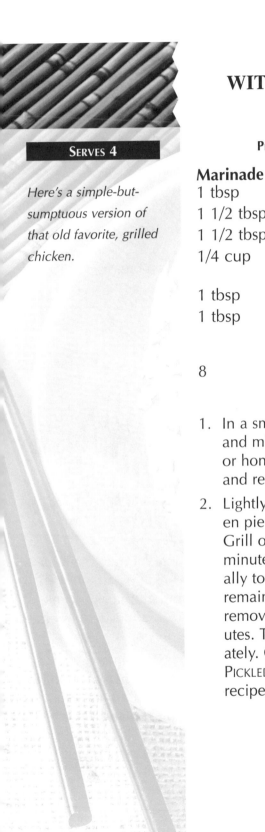

**SERVES 4**

*Here's a simple-but-sumptuous version of that old favorite, grilled chicken.*

**Preheat broiler or barbecue at medium-high**

## Marinade

| | | |
|---|---|---|
| 1 tbsp | Dijon mustard | 15 mL |
| 1 1/2 tbsp | hoisin sauce | 20 mL |
| 1 1/2 tbsp | soya sauce | 20 mL |
| 1/4 cup | frozen orange juice concentrate, thawed | 50 mL |
| 1 tbsp | minced ginger root | 15 mL |
| 1 tbsp | minced garlic | 15 mL |
| | Sugar or honey to taste | |
| 8 | chicken thighs (or 4 breasts) | 8 |
| | Orange slices for garnish (optional) | |

1. In a small bowl, combine ingredients for marinade and mix well. Adjust sweetness to taste with sugar or honey. Rub marinade evenly over chicken; cover and refrigerate for 30 minutes or overnight.

2. Lightly oil barbecue or broiler rack. Remove chicken pieces from marinade; brush off excess solids. Grill or broil until golden brown, about 8 to 10 minutes per side. Be sure to turn chicken occasionally to prevent burning and baste evenly with remaining marinade. When chicken is cooked, remove from heat and allow to rest for 2 to 3 minutes. Transfer to serving platter and serve immediately. Garnish with orange slices and, if desired, PICKLED VEGETABLES IN HONEY RICE VINEGAR (see recipe, page 78).

# STIR-FRIED VELVET CHICKEN WITH ROSEMARY GINGER AND CARROTS

**Preheat oven to 375° F (190° C)**

*The "velvet" here refers to how the Chinese interpret the smooth texture of this chicken.*

*You can substitute sage or basil for the rosemary.*

*For best results, slice the chicken as thinly as possible.*

*Finish the dish with a healthy grind of black pepper.*

## Marinade

| | | |
|---|---|---|
| 2 tbsp | cornstarch | 25 mL |
| 1 | egg white, beaten | 1 |
| 1 tbsp | minced ginger root | 15 mL |
| 1 tsp | minced rosemary | 5 mL |
| 1 lb | boneless skinless chicken breasts, thinly sliced | 500 g |
| 1 tbsp | vegetable oil | 15 mL |
| | Salt and pepper to taste | |
| 2 cups | thinly sliced carrots | 500 mL |
| 1 tsp | minced rosemary | 5 mL |
| 1 tbsp | minced ginger root | 15 mL |
| 1 tsp | sesame oil | 5 mL |
| 1 cup | chicken stock *or* water | 250 mL |
| | Salt and pepper to taste | |

1. In a large bowl, combine cornstarch, egg white, ginger root and rosemary. Add chicken; stir well. Refrigerate for 10 minutes.

2. In a nonstick wok or skillet, heat oil over high heat for 30 seconds. Add chicken mixture, season with salt and pepper and stir-fry until all traces of pink have disappeared from the meat, about 3 to 4 minutes. Transfer to a plate and set aside.

3. Return pan to stove. Add carrots, rosemary, ginger root, sesame oil and chicken stock. Increase heat to high and cook until most of the liquid has evaporated, about 5 minutes. Add chicken and stir to heat through. Season with salt and pepper. Transfer to a warm platter and serve immediately.

# PEPPER CHICKEN STIR-FRY

*The combination of Szechuan pepper and black pepper gives this dish a special depth of flavor. Try putting this combination in your pepper grinder for everyday use.*

| 1 lb | boneless chicken breast, thinly sliced | 500 g |
|------|------|------|
| 2 tsp | Szechuan peppercorns *or* dried red or green peppercorns | 10 mL |
| 2 tsp | black peppercorns | 10 mL |

**Sauce**

| 1 tbsp | cornstarch | 15 mL |
|------|------|------|
| 2 tbsp | oyster sauce | 25 mL |
| 1 tbsp | soya sauce | 15 mL |
| 2 tbsp | chicken stock | 25 mL |

| 1 tbsp | vegetable oil | 15 mL |
|------|------|------|
| 1 | small onion, thinly sliced | 1 |
| 2 tsp | minced ginger root | 10 mL |
| 2 tsp | minced garlic | 10 mL |
| 1 cup | sliced green peppers | 250 mL |
| 1 cup | sliced red bell peppers | 250 mL |

1. Combine peppercorns. Coarsely grind in a pepper grinder or mortar and pestle, or by crushing with a wine bottle between two sheets of waxed paper.

2. In a bowl combine chicken and mixed peppercorns; mix well.

3. In a small bowl, combine ingredients for sauce; set aside.

4. In a nonstick wok or skillet, heat oil over medium heat. Add onion, ginger root and garlic; fry until fragrant, about 1 minute. Push vegetables to one side of wok; add chicken and stir-fry until meat turns opaque and golden, about 3 minutes. Add bell peppers and stir-fry 1 minute. Add sauce mixture; bring to a boil and stir until sauce thickens. Transfer to a platter and serve immediately.

# SOYA-BRAISED TURKEY WITH CITRUS AND SQUASH

*This technique can be used with any boneless turkey meat — thighs, legs or breasts.*

*The process of braising, which is usually time-consuming, can be accelerated by cutting the raw turkey into bite-size chunks.*

| | | |
|---|---|---|
| 1 tbsp | vegetable oil | 15 mL |
| 1 tbsp | minced ginger root | 15 mL |
| 1 tbsp | minced garlic | 15 mL |
| 1 lb | boneless turkey, cut into 1-inch (2.5 cm) cubes | 500 g |
| 2 cups | squash, seeded, peeled and cut into 1-inch (2.5 cm) cubes | 500 mL |
| 3 cups | turkey stock *or* chicken stock | 750 mL |
| 2 tbsp | sweet soya sauce | 25 mL |
| 1 | jalapeno pepper, thinly sliced | 1 |
| 1 tbsp | honey | 15 mL |
| 1 | lemon, zest and juice | 1 |
| 1 | grapefruit, zest and juice | 1 |
| 2 tbsp | cornstarch dissolved in 4 tbsp (60 mL) water | 25 mL |
| | Salt and pepper to taste | |

1. In a nonstick skillet, heat oil over medium-high heat for 30 seconds. Add ginger root, garlic, turkey and squash; sauté until the turkey begins to brown.

2. Add stock, sweet soya sauce, jalapeno, honey and the lemon and grapefruit zest and juice; bring to a boil. Add dissolved cornstarch and stir until the mixture begins to thicken. Reduce heat and simmer until the turkey is tender and the squash is cooked, about 10 to 20 minutes. Serve with steamed rice.

# OVEN-ROASTED MAPLE GINGER CHICKEN WINGS

**SERVES 4**

*Roasting renders fat from the chicken and leaves a crispy base for the sweet-and-spicy coating.*

*For a great family dinner, serve with LEEK AND BACON FRIED RICE (see recipe, page 166) and PAN-FRIED BABY BOK CHOY WITH SESAME OIL AND GINGER (see recipe, page 145). Napkins will definitely be required!*

**Preheat oven to 375° F (190° C)**

| | | |
|---|---|---|
| 2 lbs | chicken wings | 1 kg |
| 2 tbsp | vegetable oil | 25 mL |
| 1 tbsp | minced ginger root | 15 mL |
| | Salt and pepper to taste | |

**Sauce**

| | | |
|---|---|---|
| 1 tbsp | minced orange zest | 15 mL |
| 2 tbsp | rice vinegar | 25 mL |
| 2 tbsp | maple syrup | 25 mL |
| 1 tbsp | chili paste | 15 mL |
| 1 tbsp | minced ginger root | 15 mL |

1. In a large roasting pan, combine chicken wings, vegetable oil and ginger root. Season well with salt and pepper; mix well. Roast in preheated oven 25 to 30 minutes or until the wings are golden brown. Remove from oven and transfer to a serving dish.

2. In a small bowl, combine ingredients for sauce. Mix well, pour over chicken and toss until thoroughly combined.

# BARBECUED DUCK AND WATERCRESS ROLLS WITH GINGER PLUM COMPOTE

SERVES 4 TO 6

*If you don't fancy duck, try roasted chicken, turkey or pork — they all make great substitutes in this simple but delicious recipe.*

### Ginger Plum Compote

| | | |
|---|---|---|
| 4 or 5 | large black plums | 4 or 5 |
| 1/2 cup | white wine | 125 mL |
| 2 tbsp | sugar | 25 mL |
| 2 tsp | cider vinegar | 10 mL |
| 2 tsp | grated ginger root | 10 mL |
| | Salt and pepper to taste | |
| 1 | barbecued duck *or* 1 lb (500 g) roasted poultry or pork | 1 |
| 12 | 6-inch (15 cm) flour tortillas | 12 |
| 1 | large bunch watercress, trimmed, washed and spun dry | 1 |

1. With a sharp knife, cut plums in half and remove pits; cut each pitted half into 4 wedges.

2. In a non-reactive saucepan over medium heat, bring ingredients for compote to a boil. Cook 10 minutes, stirring frequently. Season to taste with salt and pepper; add more sugar if required. Allow to cool to room temperature; transfer to a serving bowl. (The recipe can be prepared to this point up to 2 days ahead.)

3. With a sharp knife, carve meat from duck and slice into thin slices.

4. In a dry skillet, briefly toast each tortilla until warm.

5. To serve: Arrange duck slices on a platter with watercress leaves, plum compote and tortillas. Allow diners to assemble their own rolls by spreading 1 tbsp (15 mL) compote on the tortilla, topping with watercress and duck, then rolling up the tortilla fajita-style.

# MEAT

# ORANGE GINGER GARLIC BEEF

*Dry orange or tangerine peel is available in Asian markets. If it's stored in a tightly sealed container it will last indefinitely. Don't buy the cheapest version as good quality peel delivers better results.*

*For a great finish, try using CANDIED PECANS (see recipe, page 170) as a garnish.*

| | | |
|---|---|---|
| 1 1/2 lbs | lean beef, cut into thin strips | 750 g |
| 5 | pieces dried orange peel *or* 2 tsp (10 mL) orange zest and 2 tbsp (25 mL) frozen orange juice concentrate, thawed | 5 |
| 7 or 8 | broccoli florets (optional) | 7 or 8 |
| 1/3 cup | sugar | 75 mL |
| 1/3 cup | red wine vinegar *or* Chinese black vinegar | 75 mL |
| 1 tsp | salt | 5 mL |
| 1 tbsp | dark soya sauce | 15 mL |
| 1/4 cup | cornstarch | 50 mL |
| 2 cups | vegetable oil for deep frying | 500 mL |
| 3 tbsp | grated ginger root | 45 mL |
| 1 1/2 tbsp | minced garlic | 20 mL |

1. Spread beef on a baking sheet lined with paper towels and allow to dry thoroughly in refrigerator for 30 minutes.

2. In a small bowl, soak orange peel (if using) in 2 tbsp (25 mL) warm water for 5 minutes or until just soft. Drain, reserving liquid; set aside.

3. If using, blanch broccoli in boiling salted water for 2 minutes. Set aside.

4. In a small bowl, combine sugar, vinegar, orange peel liquid or orange juice concentrate, salt and soya sauce; mix well. Set aside.

5. In a plastic bag, toss beef with cornstarch until thoroughly coated.

6. In a wok over medium-high heat, heat oil until just smoking. Fry beef in batches until crispy golden brown, about 3 minutes. With a slotted spoon, transfer beef onto a paper towel and keep warm.

7. Drain all but 1 tbsp (15 mL) oil from wok. Add orange peel or zest, ginger root and garlic; cook briefly to extract flavors. Add vinegar-soya mixture; bring to a boil and cook until the sauce becomes caramelized and syrupy in appearance. Adjust seasoning to taste with salt and pepper. Add beef, stirring vigorously, until well coated. Serve immediately, garnished with broccoli florets, if desired.

*Flank steak, is juicy and flavorful, and it's great in stir-fry dishes. Slice it across the grain and it will be tender when cooked.*

# SAUTÉED BEEF WITH ASPARAGUS IN OYSTER SAUCE

| | | |
|---|---|---|
| 1/2 tsp | black peppercorns | 2 mL |
| 1/2 tsp | Szechuan peppercorns *or* green or red peppercorns | 2 mL |

**Sauce**

| | | |
|---|---|---|
| 2 tbsp | oyster sauce | 25 mL |
| 1 tbsp | soya sauce | 15 mL |
| 1 tbsp | chicken stock *or* water | 15 mL |
| 2 tsp | cornstarch | 10 mL |
| | | |
| 2 tbsp | vegetable oil | 25 mL |
| 2 tsp | minced ginger root | 10 mL |
| 2 tsp | minced garlic | 10 mL |
| 1 | small onion, sliced | 1 |
| 12 oz | flank steak, thinly sliced across the grain | 375 g |
| 1 lb | asparagus, cut into 2-inch (5 cm) segments | 500 g |

1. Combine peppercorns. Coarsely grind in a pepper grinder, mortar and pestle, or by crushing with a wine bottle between two sheets of waxed paper.

2. In a small bowl, combine ingredients for sauce; mix well and set aside.

3. In a nonstick wok or skillet, heat oil over medium-high heat for 30 seconds. Add ginger root, garlic and onion; stir-fry 1 minute or until fragrant. Add beef; cook, stirring to separate pieces, about 2 minutes. Season with mixed peppercorns. Add asparagus; toss to mix and cook 2 minutes. Add sauce mixture; stir and cook until thickened. Transfer to a serving platter and serve immediately.

ORANGE GINGER GARLIC BEEF (PAGE 126) ➤

*OVERLEAF:* STIR-FRIED CHICKEN WITH PEACHES AND PICKLED GINGER (PAGE 116)

# STEWED BEEF WITH WHOLE GARLIC, HOISIN AND BARLEY

*This hearty dish is a great cool-weather warmer.*

*Refrigerating overnight actually helps to develop the flavor of this stew. Reheat on top of the stove, over medium-low heat, stirring occasionally to prevent the stew from sticking and thin with additional stock or water, if required.*

| | | |
|---|---|---|
| 4 tbsp | all-purpose flour | 60 mL |
| | Salt and pepper to taste | |
| 1 lb | stewing beef, cut into 1-inch (2.5 cm) cubes | 500 g |
| 1 tbsp | vegetable oil | 15 mL |
| 1 | medium onion, cut into 1/2-inch (1 cm) dice | 1 |
| 1 | head garlic, cloves peeled | 1 |
| 2 | medium carrots, cut into 1-inch (2.5 cm) dice | 2 |
| 1 cup | pearl barley | 250 mL |
| 6 cups | beef stock | 1.5 L |
| 3 tbsp | hoisin sauce | 45 mL |
| 1 tbsp | dark soya sauce | 15 mL |
| 1 tsp | chili sauce | 5 mL |
| 1 tbsp | chopped cilantro | 15 mL |
| | Salt and pepper to taste | |

1. In a plastic bag, combine flour, salt and pepper. Add beef and shake until thoroughly coated.

2. In a large pot, heat oil over high heat for 30 seconds. Add dredged beef and stir-fry until the meat begins to brown, about 5 minutes. Add onion, garlic, carrots and barley; cook for 3 minutes. Add beef stock, hoisin sauce, soya sauce, chili sauce and cilantro; bring to a boil. Reduce heat and simmer 40 minutes or until beef is tender and the barley is soft. Season with salt and pepper. Serve over steamed rice or mashed potatoes.

◄ ROCK SALT PAN-ROASTED CHICKEN IN GARLIC SESAME AND OLIVE OIL (PAGE 112)

# STIR-FRIED SALT-AND-PEPPER BEEF WITH CHINESE GREENS

*Surprisingly, the simple seasonings — salt, pepper and soya — in this dish really bring out the flavor of beef. We've eaten somewhat similar versions in Chinese restaurants where it's described as "Mongolian Beef."*

*For a vegetarian alternative, try substituting large shiitake or portobello mushrooms for the beef.*

### Beef Marinade

| | | |
|---|---|---|
| 1 cup | white wine | 250 mL |
| 1 lb | sirloin beef, thinly sliced | 500 g |
| 2 tbsp | cornstarch | 25 mL |
| 1 tsp | salt | 5 mL |
| 1 tsp | freshly ground black pepper | 5 mL |

### Sauce

| | | |
|---|---|---|
| 2 tbsp | vegetable oil, divided | 25 mL |
| 1 | onion, peeled and thinly sliced | 1 |
| 1 tbsp | minced garlic | 15 mL |
| 1 cup | beef stock | 250 mL |
| 1 tbsp | dark soya sauce | 15 mL |
| 2 tbsp | cornstarch dissolved in 4 tbsp (60 mL) water | 25 mL |
| 3 cups | chopped Chinese greens (bok choy, *sui choy*, gailan, mustard, etc.) | 750 mL |
| | Freshly ground black pepper to taste | |

1. In a large glass or ceramic bowl, combine white wine and beef; stir to coat. Add cornstarch, salt and pepper; mix well. Chill for 30 minutes.

2. With a slotted spoon, remove meat from the marinade. Set liquid aside.

3. In a nonstick wok or skillet, heat 1 tbsp (15 mL) oil over high heat for 45 seconds. Add beef; stir-fry until it begins to brown and no red is visible, about 2 to 3 minutes. Transfer to a warm plate. Set aside.

4. Return pan to high heat. Add remaining 1 tbsp (15 mL) oil and heat for 30 seconds. Add onion and garlic; stir-fry until onion begins to soften. Add beef stock and soya sauce; bring to a boil. Add reserved marinade and bring to a boil. Add dissolved cornstarch; return to a boil, stirring to thicken. Add Chinese greens and stir until they just begin to wilt. Return beef to pan and stir to heat through, about 2 minutes. Transfer to a warm platter and serve with steamed rice or mashed potatoes.

# Baked Ginger Beef and Vegetable Balls with Oyster and Mushroom Sauce

*In this delicious and hearty dish, roasted meat balls are coated in a rich sauce of mushrooms and oyster sauce.*

*You can make this dish up to 6 hours in advance. Reheat in a 375° F (190° C) oven for 10 to 15 minutes. If the mixture thickens too much, simply add more stock or water.*

**Preheat oven to 375° F (190° C)**

**Oiled baking sheet**

## Meatballs

| | | |
|---|---|---|
| 2 | slices day-old bread | 2 |
| 1 lb | lean ground beef | 500 g |
| 1 tbsp | minced ginger root | 15 mL |
| 1 tsp | sesame oil | 5 mL |
| 1 cup | *sui choy* (Napa cabbage), finely chopped | 250 mL |
| | Salt and pepper to taste | |

## Sauce

| | | |
|---|---|---|
| 1 tbsp | vegetable oil | 15 mL |
| 1 lb | mixed mushrooms (button, shiitake, oyster, portobello, etc.), sliced | 500 g |
| 1 tbsp | minced garlic | 15 mL |
| 1 tsp | sesame oil | 5 mL |
| 2 tbsp | oyster sauce | 25 mL |
| 2 cups | beef stock | 500 mL |
| 2 tbsp | cornstarch dissolved in 4 tbsp (60 mL) water | 25 mL |

1. In a small bowl, combine bread and enough hot water to cover; let sit for 10 minutes. Pour off excess water and gently squeeze to remove most of the moisture.

2. In a large mixing bowl, combine moist bread with ground beef, ginger root, sesame oil and cabbage. Use your hands to work the mixture into a smooth paste. Chill for 10 minutes.

3. Form beef into balls, approximately 1 inch (2.5 cm) in diameter, and place on oiled baking sheet. Roast in preheated oven for 15 minutes or until the meatballs are browned. Remove from oven and keep warm while you make the sauce.

4. In a nonstick wok or skillet, heat oil over high heat for 30 seconds. Add mushrooms and garlic; stir and cook until the mushrooms are soft and their liquid has evaporated, about 5 minutes.

5. Add sesame oil, oyster sauce and stock; bring to a boil. Add dissolved cornstarch and stir until mixture thickens. Add meatballs, mix well and transfer to a serving bowl or platter.

# WOK-SEARED BEEF TENDERLOIN WITH MUSHROOMS AND CHAR SUI SAUCE

**SERVES 4**

*This is a heavenly combination — tender and juicy slices of beef tenderloin with mush-rooms, wrapped in a tangy sauce. Just add steamed rice or mashed potatoes for a special treat.*

| | | |
|---|---|---|
| 1 lb | beef tenderloin, cut into slices 1/2 inch (1 cm) thick | 500 g |
| 4 tbsp | cornstarch | 60 mL |
| | Salt and pepper to taste | |

**Sauce**

| | | |
|---|---|---|
| 2 tbsp | vegetable oil, divided | 25 mL |
| 1 | medium onion, thinly sliced | 1 |
| 1 tbsp | minced garlic | 15 mL |
| 1 tbsp | minced ginger root | 15 mL |
| 1 tsp | chili sauce | 5 mL |
| 1 lb | button mushrooms, thinly sliced | 500 g |
| 8 oz | baby bok choy *or* broccoli | 250 g |
| 2 tbsp | *char sui* sauce *or* barbecue sauce | 25 mL |
| 1 1/2 cups | beef stock | 375 mL |
| 2 tbsp | cornstarch, dissolved in 4 tbsp (60 mL) water | 25 mL |
| | Salt and pepper to taste | |

1. In a plastic bag, combine cornstarch, salt and pep-per. Add beef and shake to coat well.

2. In a nonstick wok or skillet, heat 1 tbsp (15 mL) oil over medium-high heat for 30 seconds. Add beef and fry until browned but still rare, about 3 minutes per side. Transfer to a warm plate and set aside.

3. Return wok to burner and heat remaining oil over high heat for 30 seconds. Add onion, garlic, ginger root and chili sauce; stir-fry until onion begins to soften, about 2 to 3 minutes. Add mushrooms, turn heat to high and sauté for 5 minutes or until mush-rooms are soft. Add bok choy, *char sui* (or barbecue sauce) and beef stock. Stir well and bring to a boil. Add dissolved cornstarch and stir to thicken.

4. Return the beef to wok, stir and heat to warm through. Season with salt and pepper. Serve with steamed rice or mashed potatoes.

# PLUM AND CHILI GLAZED PORK TENDERLOIN

*Pork tenderloin is a lean and flavorful meat that can be rapidly cooked to moist perfection.*

*Since plum sauce has a high sugar content, it will tend to burn; be prepared to lower the heat if the meat starts to brown too quickly.*

*This dish is delicious served over SPINACH, SUNFLOWER SEED AND GARLIC SAUTÉ (see recipe, page 151).*

*You can cook the spinach in the same pan as the meat — just add some steamed rice for a complete meal.*

| | | |
|---|---|---|
| 1 lb | pork tenderloin, cut into 1/2-inch (1 cm) slices | 500 g |
| 1 tbsp | olive oil | 15 mL |
| 1 tbsp | TOASTED CHILI OIL (see recipe, page 36) | 15 mL |
| 1 tsp | chili sauce | 5 mL |
| 2 tbsp | plum sauce | 25 mL |
| | Salt and pepper to taste | |

SPINACH, SUNFLOWER SEED AND GARLIC SAUTÉ, *optional* (see recipe, page 151)

1. In a bowl combine pork, olive oil, chili oil, chili sauce and plum sauce. Mix well and set aside for 5 minutes.

2. Heat a nonstick skillet over medium-high heat for 30 seconds. Add pork and cook until the bottom is seared and starting to brown, about 4 minutes per side. Reduce heat if the mixture browns too quickly. When pork is cooked through, remove from heat and serve over SPINACH, SUNFLOWER SEED AND GARLIC SAUTÉ or with a vegetable of your choice.

# STIR-FRIED PORK
# WITH GARLIC CHIVES

**SERVES 4**

*This simple stir-fry is a popular dish in both restaurants and homes in China.*

## Pork and Marinade

| | | |
|---|---|---|
| 12 oz | lean pork loin, cut into thin strips | 375 g |
| 1 tbsp | soya sauce | 15 mL |
| 1 tbsp | dark soya sauce | 15 mL |
| 1 tbsp | oyster sauce | 15 mL |
| 1/2 tsp | freshly ground black pepper | 2 mL |
| 1/4 tsp | sugar | 1 mL |
| 1 tbsp | cornstarch | 15 mL |
| | | |
| 1 tbsp | vegetable oil | 15 mL |
| 2 | cloves garlic, minced | 2 |
| 2 cups | garlic (Chinese) chives, cut into 2-inch (5 cm) pieces *or* thinly sliced leeks | 500 mL |
| 2 tbsp | dry sherry | 25 mL |
| 2 cups | bean sprouts | 500 mL |
| 2 tsp | sesame oil | 10 mL |

1. In a bowl combine pork with marinade ingredients and mix well. Set aside to marinate for 20 minutes.

2. Heat wok or heavy skillet over high heat; add oil and heat until just smoking. Add pork and garlic; stir-fry for 2 minutes or until pork is just cooked. Add chives and stir-fry for 30 seconds. Splash with sherry; cover and cook for 1 minute. Add bean sprouts and sesame oil; stir-fry for 1 minute. Transfer to a platter and serve immediately.

# PAN-FRIED PORK CHOPS WITH SUN-DRIED TOMATOES AND CILANTRO

*Here's a great way to use supermarket pork chops. Without the chili flakes, they make great pork fingers, which most kids love.*

*The best way to cut dehydrated tomatoes is with kitchen shears, but you can also reconstitute them first by soaking in boiling water for a couple of minutes, then chopping them with a heavy knife.*

*If you can't get thin pork chops, use 3 thicker butterfly chops cut in half horizontally. Then cut each slice into 3 or 4 pieces.*

| | | |
|---|---|---|
| 6 | boneless pork chops, cut into very thin slices | 6 |
| 1/4 cup | all-purpose flour | 50 mL |
| 1 tbsp | cornstarch | 15 mL |
| 2 tsp | seasoned salt | 10 mL |
| 1 cup | vegetable oil | 250 mL |
| 2 tbsp | finely chopped sun-dried tomatoes | 25 mL |
| 2 tbsp | finely chopped shallots | 25 mL |
| 2 tsp | minced garlic | 10 mL |
| 1 tsp | dried chili flakes (optional) | 5 mL |
| 2 tbsp | dry sherry *or* Chinese *shaoxing* wine | 25 mL |
| 2 tbsp | chopped cilantro | 25 mL |

1. Pat pork dry with paper towels. Using a heavy knife, cut each pork chop into 3 or 4 pieces. Combine flour, cornstarch and salt in a plastic bag and shake to mix well. Divide pork chops into 2 or 3 batches; add to flour mixture and toss until well coated.

2. Heat oil in a wok or heavy skillet over medium-high heat. Shake off excess coating from floured pork pieces and fry until golden, about 2 to 3 minutes per side. Drain well and keep warm. Repeat until all pork is cooked.

3. Drain all but 1 tbsp (15 mL) oil from wok. Add tomatoes, shallots, garlic and chili flakes, if using; stir-fry for 1 minute or until fragrant. Add pork and stir to mix well. Splash with wine and toss until liquid is absorbed. Add cilantro and toss to mix. Transfer to a platter and serve immediately.

# BRAISED ROASTED PORK WITH TOFU AND GREEN ONIONS

*Crispy-skinned and suc-culent roasted pork, sold by the pound, is one of our favorite treats from the Chinese barbecue shop. It's hard not to eat it right away, but if there's anything left, this is a great way to use it up.*

| | | |
|---|---|---|
| 4 | dried Chinese black mushrooms | 4 |
| 1 lb | Crispy-skin roasted pork *or* barbecued pork *or* leftover roast pork, cut into 1/2-inch (1 cm) slices | 500 g |
| 1 tbsp | vegetable oil | 15 mL |
| 5 | thin slices ginger root | 5 |
| 1 tsp | minced garlic | 5 mL |
| 2 tbsp | oyster sauce | 25 mL |
| 1 tbsp | soya sauce | 15 mL |
| 1 tbsp | dark soya sauce | 15 mL |
| 1/2 cup | chicken stock *or* water | 125 mL |
| | Salt and freshly ground black pepper to taste | |
| 1 tbsp | cornstarch, dissolved in 2 tbsp (25 mL) chicken stock *or* water | 15 mL |
| 2 | packages (10 oz [300 g]) soft tofu, cut into pieces 1 inch (2.5 cm) by 1/2 inch (1 cm) | 2 |
| 3 | green onions, cut into 1-inch (2.5 cm) lengths | 3 |

1. In a heatproof bowl, soak mushrooms in boiling water for 15 minutes. Remove stems, slice caps thinly and set aside.

2. In a wok or deep skillet, heat oil over medium-high heat. Add ginger root, garlic and mushrooms and sauté until fragrant (about 1 minute). Add pork and stir-fry for 1 minute. Add oyster sauce, soya sauces and stock; mix well, reduce heat to medium and cook for 3 minutes. Season to taste with salt and pepper. Add dissolved cornstarch and cook until sauce is thickened.

3. Gently fold tofu and green onions into mixture; cover and allow to absorb flavors for 2 minutes. Transfer to a deep platter and serve immediately.

# WESTERN-STYLE MONGOLIAN LAMB CHOPS

**Preheat oven to 400° F (200° C)**

**Ovenproof skillet *or* shallow roasting pan**

*This "fusion" recipe combines condiments from a Mongolian lamb fire-pot-dinner with western herbs and French cooking techniques. We've used a dark sesame paste, which is available in Asian markets, but if you can't find it, light sesame paste or tahini from the Greek or Mediterranean section of your supermarket makes a satisfactory substitute.*

## Marinade

| | | |
|---|---|---|
| 1 tbsp | finely chopped thyme | 15 mL |
| 1 tbsp | finely chopped rosemary | 15 mL |
| 2 | cloves garlic, minced | 2 |
| 1/4 tsp | salt | 1 mL |
| 1/4 tsp | freshly ground black pepper | 1 mL |
| 1 tbsp | olive oil | 15 mL |
| 12 | lamb chops, about 3/4 inch (2 cm) thick, trimmed | 12 |

## Sauce

| | | |
|---|---|---|
| 1 cup | red wine | 250 mL |
| 2 tbsp | oyster sauce | 25 mL |
| 1 tbsp | hoisin sauce | 15 mL |
| 1 tbsp | chili bean sauce (or to taste) | 15 mL |
| 1 tbsp | dark sesame paste *or* tahini | 15 mL |

1. In a small bowl, combine ingredients for marinade; mix well. Rub marinade on chops and set aside to marinate in the refrigerator for 2 hours or overnight.

2. Heat a large skillet, preferably ovenproof, over medium-high heat. Sear lamb chops until golden brown, about 1 minute per side. Place in preheated oven and cook for 10 minutes. (If you don't have an ovenproof skillet, set aside skillet in which the chops were seared and transfer meat to a shallow roasting pan; when lamb is cooked, pour accumulated juices into the skillet and proceed with the recipe.) Transfer meat to a warm platter and allow to rest while finishing preparation of the sauce.

3. Add wine to skillet and cook over high heat until reduced by half. Strain through a fine sieve into a small saucepan. Add oyster sauce, hoisin sauce, chili bean sauce and sesame paste; stir to mix and heat through. Pour over lamb chops and serve.

# Roast Leg of Lamb with Sweet Soya Rosemary Gravy

*This is a great dish for family dinners. The gravy is wonderful with mashed potatoes, baked potatoes or rice.*

*Make sure your lamb has been trimmed so there's only a thin cap of fat. If you don't like lamb, try making this with beef or pork — both work well.*

*Serve this dish with Five-Spice and Spinach Scalloped Potatoes (see recipe, page 154) or Mashed Potatoes with Ginger Green Onion Pesto (see recipe, page 156) and steamed vegetables.*

**Preheat oven to 375° F (190° C)**
**Large roasting pan**

| | | |
|---|---|---|
| 1 tbsp | vegetable oil | 15 mL |
| 1 tbsp | minced garlic | 15 mL |
| 1 tbsp | minced rosemary | 15 mL |
| | Salt and pepper to taste | |
| 2 lbs | boneless leg of lamb | 1 kg |

**Gravy**

| | | |
|---|---|---|
| 4 tbsp | all-purpose flour | 60 mL |
| 1 tbsp | minced rosemary | 15 mL |
| 1 tbsp | minced garlic | 15 mL |
| 2 cups | beef stock | 500 mL |
| 1 tbsp | sweet soya sauce or Sweet Soya Substitute (see recipe, page 34) | 15 mL |
| | Salt and pepper to taste | |

1. In a small bowl, combine oil, garlic, rosemary, salt and pepper. Rub mixture over lamb and roast in preheated oven until the surface is golden brown and crusty. If you like your meat rare, allow about 40 minutes; for well done, expect 60 minutes.

2. Remove roast from the oven; place on a serving platter and keep warm.

3. Pour pan juices into a measuring cup. You'll need 4 tbsp (60 mL). If you have more, pour off excess; if you don't have enough, add vegetable oil to make up the required amount. Return juices to the pan; stir in flour, rosemary and garlic, ensuring that all the flour is absorbed. Cook, stirring, over medium-high heat until the mixture begins to brown.

4. Add half the beef stock slowly to the pan and whisk until mixture begins to thicken. Whisk in the rest of the stock along with the sweet soya sauce. Reduce heat and simmer for 5 minutes.

5. To serve: With your sharpest knife, slice the lamb thinly. Pour accumulated juices back into the sauce, stir to combine, then pour over the sliced lamb.

# VEGETABLES

# PEA TOPS WITH PANCETTA AND TOFU

*Pea tops are the shoots of snow pea plants. They're now available almost year round in Asian markets. They are tasty in salads and have a subtle, nutty flavor when cooked. However, they are quite perishable and won't last much longer than a couple of days in your refrigerator.*

| | | |
|---|---|---|
| 1 | 3-inch (7.5 cm) square medium tofu | 1 |
| 2 tbsp | vegetable oil, divided | 25 mL |
| | Salt and pepper to taste | |
| 1 tsp | sesame oil | 5 mL |
| 2 | slices pancetta or prosciutto, finely chopped | 2 |
| 2 tsp | minced garlic | 10 mL |
| 8 oz | pea tops *or* arugula | 250 g |
| 2 tbsp | chicken stock *or* vegetable stock | 25 mL |

1. Slice tofu into pieces 1/2 inch (1 cm) thick by 1 1/2 inches (3.5 cm) square.

2. In a nonstick skillet, heat 1 tbsp (15 mL) oil over medium-high heat for 30 seconds. Add tofu and season lightly with salt, pepper and sesame oil; fry until golden, about 1 minute per side. Remove from skillet; arrange on a platter and keep warm.

3. Add remaining oil to skillet and heat for 30 seconds. Add pancetta and garlic; fry briefly until fragrant, about 20 to 30 seconds. Add pea tops and stock; stir-fry until pea tops are just wilted. Arrange evenly over tofu and serve.

# Braised Shanghai Bok Choy with Oyster Mushrooms and Garlic

*Prized for its tender texture, Shanghai bok choy is a close cousin of regular bok choy, with spoon-shaped leaves and thinner stalks on the same bulbous base. The main difference is its color — a paler green than regular bok choy. It's sold in bundles of 4 to 5 heads and is at its best when no more than 5 or 6 inches (12.5 or 15 cm) tall.*

**Sauce**

| | | |
|---|---|---|
| 1 tbsp | cornstarch | 15 mL |
| 1 tsp | sesame oil | 5 mL |
| 1 tbsp | oyster sauce | 15 mL |
| 1 tbsp | chicken stock | 15 mL |
| | | |
| 1 tbsp | vegetable oil | 15 mL |
| 2 cups | oyster mushrooms, torn into bite-sized pieces | 500 mL |
| 1 tsp | minced garlic | 5 mL |
| 1 tsp | minced ginger root | 5 mL |
| 4 | medium Shanghai bok choy or regular bok choy, cut lengthwise into quarters | 4 |
| 1/3 cup | chicken stock | 75 mL |
| | Salt and pepper to taste | |

1. In a small bowl, combine ingredients for sauce; mix well and set aside.

2. In a wok or deep skillet, heat oil over medium-high heat for about 30 seconds. Add mushrooms, garlic and ginger root; sauté until mushrooms are golden, about 1 to 2 minutes. Add bok choy; toss and cook briefly. Add chicken stock; bring to boil. Turn heat to low; cover and allow to braise for 2 to 3 minutes or until vegetables are tender.

3. Stir in sauce ingredients and cook until slightly thickened. Season to taste with salt and pepper. Transfer to a platter and serve immediately.

# PAN-FRIED BABY BOK CHOY WITH SESAME OIL AND GINGER

*Bok choy, a juicy and refreshing Chinese white cabbage, is also packed with vitamins and nutrients. For additional flavor, cook this dish in the same pan in which your meat or fish has been cooked.*

| | | |
|---|---|---|
| 1 lb | baby bok choy | 500 g |
| 1 tbsp | vegetable oil | 15 mL |
| 1 tbsp | minced ginger root | 15 mL |
| 3 tbsp | water *or* chicken stock | 45 mL |
| 1 tsp | sesame oil | 5 mL |
| | Salt and pepper to taste | |

1. With a heavy knife, cut bok choy across the bottom to separate stems. Cut each stem in half lengthwise and wash thoroughly.

2. In a nonstick pan, heat oil for 30 seconds. Add ginger root and sauté until fragrant, about 1 minute. Add bok choy and cook until it begins to color and the leaves turn bright green, about 2 to 3 minutes. Add water or stock and sesame oil; cook until all the liquid has evaporated.

3. Transfer to a platter, season with salt and pepper and serve immediately.

# Grilled Asparagus with Lemon Honey Soya Butter

**SERVES 4**

*If you like lemon chicken, you'll love this.*

**Preheat broiler or start barbecue**

| | | |
|---|---|---|
| 2 tbsp | fresh lemon juice | 25 mL |
| 2 tbsp | honey | 25 mL |
| 1 tbsp | soya sauce | 15 mL |
| 2 tbsp | butter, chilled | 25 mL |
| 16 to 20 | asparagus spears, trimmed and washed | 16 to 20 |
| 1 tbsp | sesame oil | 15 mL |
| | Salt and pepper to taste | |

1. In a small saucepan, heat lemon juice, honey and soya sauce over medium heat for 1 minute. Whisk in chilled butter until slightly creamy. Adjust sweetness with additional honey, if desired. Set aside.

2. Brush asparagus with sesame oil until coated. Barbecue or broil until tender, 1 to 2 minutes per side. Season with salt and pepper; cover with sauce and serve.

# STIR-FRIED ASPARAGUS WITH GARLIC, SHALLOTS AND TOASTED CHILI OIL

SERVES 4

*In season, this combination of asparagus, garlic and chili makes a wonderful spring treat. The water or stock steams the asparagus to a tender crispness. If you like spicy food, add dried chili flakes along with the shallots.*

| | | |
|---|---|---|
| 2 tbsp | TOASTED CHILI OIL (see recipe, page 36) | 25 mL |
| 4 | medium shallots, thinly sliced | 4 |
| 1 tbsp | minced garlic | 15 mL |
| 1 lb | asparagus, trimmed and cut into 2-inch (5 cm) lengths | 500 g |
| 3 tbsp | water *or* chicken stock | 45 mL |
| | Salt and pepper to taste | |

1. Heat a nonstick wok or skillet over high heat for 30 seconds. Add chili oil, shallots and garlic; sauté 2 minutes or until the shallots are soft and beginning to color. Add asparagus and continue to cook until it begins to soften and color, about 2 to 3 minutes.

2. Add water or stock; continue to cook until all the moisture has evaporated. Season with salt and pepper and toss to mix well. Transfer to a warm platter and serve immediately.

# Gailan in Anchovy Garlic Butter

*Commonly known as Chinese broccoli, gailan is one of our favorite greens. It has a rich, almost nutty flavor, with a slight hint of bitterness. Its dull, waxy, jade green stems and leaves turn an attractive deep green when cooked. Look for stems that are between 1/4 to 3/4 inch (5 mm to 1.5 cm) in diameter and about 6 to 8 inches (15 cm to 20 cm) in length with healthy-looking bud clusters or white flowers at the top.*

| | | |
|---|---|---|
| 1 lb | gailan *or* broccoli | 500 g |
| 2 tbsp | butter | 25 mL |
| 2 or 3 | anchovy fillets, finely chopped | 2 or 3 |
| 2 tsp | minced garlic | 10 mL |
| 1 tbsp | chicken stock | 15 mL |
| | Salt and pepper to taste | |
| 1 tbsp | toasted sesame seeds | 15 mL |

1. With a sharp knife, cut gailan horizontally into 2-inch (5 cm) segments. If stem is too thick, cut lengthwise in half before cutting into segments. If using broccoli, cut into bite-size florets.

2. In a nonstick wok or skillet, melt butter over medium heat. Add anchovies and garlic; stir-fry for 15 seconds. Add gailan or broccoli; stir until well coated. Add chicken stock; cover and cook until tender crisp, about 2 minutes. Season with salt and pepper. Transfer to serving platter; sprinkle with sesame seeds and serve.

# STEAMED GAILAN WITH OLIVE OIL AND BALSAMIC VINEGAR

*Gailan can always be purchased in Chinese markets and in supermarkets with a good Asian food section. If it isn't available, broccoli, rapini or kale make good substitutes.*

*Gailan stems are sometimes quite large. In this case, speed the cooking process by splitting them lengthwise. Be careful not to overcook or gailan will turn a drab olive color and acquire a bitter taste.*

| | | |
|---|---|---|
| 2 cups | water | 500 mL |
| 4 | slices ginger root | 4 |
| 1 lb | gailan, cut into 2-inch (5 cm) pieces, *or* broccoli florets | 500 g |
| 2 tbsp | extra virgin olive oil | 25 mL |
| 1 tbsp | balsamic vinegar | 15 mL |
| | Salt and pepper to taste | |
| | Toasted sesame seeds for garnish | |

1. In a wok or the bottom of a steamer, bring water and ginger slices to a boil. Cover with a steamer tray (or bamboo steamer); add gailan or broccoli and cover with lid. Steam 7 to 8 minutes or until the gailan is tender and bright green.

2. Transfer to a platter and top with the olive oil and balsamic vinegar. Season with salt and pepper; toss to combine. Sprinkle with sesame seeds and serve immediately.

# SPINACH, SUNFLOWER SEED AND GARLIC SAUTÉ

*Spinach is high in both iron and calcium — and it is full of wholesome flavor. Cook spinach just until leaves begin to wilt, but are still bright green.*

| 1 tbsp | vegetable oil | 15 mL |
| 1 tbsp | minced garlic | 15 mL |
| 8 oz | spinach, trimmed and washed | 250 g |
| 2 tbsp | water | 25 mL |
| 1 tsp | sesame oil | 5 mL |
| | Salt and pepper to taste | |
| 1 cup | toasted sunflower seeds | 250 mL |

1. In a nonstick pan, heat oil for 30 seconds. Add garlic and sauté until soft and beginning to color, about 2 minutes. Add spinach and sauté until it begins to soften and wilt, about 1 minute. Add water and continue to cook until it evaporates.

2. Drizzle spinach with sesame oil and season with salt and pepper. Add sunflower seeds; toss well. Transfer spinach to a warm platter and serve immediately.

# BUDDHA'S DELIGHT BLACK BEAN SAUTÉ

*In this versatile vegetarian dish, the pungent, salty flavor of black beans highlights tender-crisp vegetables.*

*Feel free to add more black bean sauce or to raise the heat by adding chili sauce to taste.*

*Most seasonal vegetables can be substituted for the cabbage or zucchini — in the winter, small cubes of squash or pumpkin make a great alternative.*

| | | |
|---|---|---|
| 1 tbsp | vegetable oil | 15 mL |
| 1 tbsp | minced garlic | 15 mL |
| 1 cup | peeled, thinly sliced carrots | 250 mL |
| 2 | small zucchini, cut into 1/2-inch (1 cm) dice | 2 |
| 1 | small *sui choy* (Napa cabbage), shredded | 1 |
| 4 | thinly sliced green onions | 4 |
| 2 tbsp | black bean sauce | 25 mL |
| 1/2 cup | vegetable stock *or* water | 125 mL |
| 1 tbsp | cornstarch dissolved in in 2 tbsp (25 mL) water | 15 mL |
| | Freshly ground black pepper to taste | |

1. In a nonstick pan over medium-high, heat oil for 30 seconds. Add garlic and cook until soft and fragrant, about 1 minute. Add carrots, zucchini and *sui choy*; cook until vegetables soften, about 2 minutes.

2. Add black bean sauce and stock to mixture; stir well and bring to a boil. Make a well in the center of the vegetables and add the dissolved cornstarch. Stir until the mixture begins to thicken; toss with vegetables. Transfer to a platter and serve immediately.

# PUMPKIN AND LOTUS ROOT STEW

| | | |
|---|---|---|
| 5 | large dried Chinese black mushrooms | 5 |
| 2 | strips bacon, chopped | 2 |
| 1 tbsp | chopped shallots | 15 mL |
| 1 tsp | minced garlic | 5 mL |
| 3 cups | pumpkin or squash flesh cut into 1-inch (2.5 cm) cubes | 750 mL |
| 1 | 6-inch (15 cm) piece lotus root *or* 4-inch (10 cm) length *daikon* radish, cut crosswise into 1/4-inch (5 mm) thick slices | 1 |
| 1 cup | chicken stock | 250 mL |
| 1 tbsp | dark soya sauce | 15 mL |
| 1 tbsp | oyster sauce | 15 mL |
| 2 | green onions, cut into 2-inch (5 cm) lengths | 2 |
| 1 tbsp | cornstarch dissolved in mushroom liquid | 15 mL |
| | Salt and pepper to taste | |

*Practically every part of the lotus plant is used in China: The flower is admired for its beauty; the leaves are used for wrapping food; the seeds are made into a sweet filling for desserts; and the lotus root is used in stews and stir-fries. Many western chefs have now taken to slicing the dramatic looking root into paper-thin slices and deep-frying them to use as a garnish.*

*While buying lotus roots, look for those that are plump, heavy, beige in color and free of blemishes.*

1.  In a heatproof bowl, soak mushrooms in 1/2 cup (125 mL) boiling water for 15 minutes. Drain and reserve liquid. Remove stems; slice caps diagonally in half and set aside.

2.  Heat a wok or deep skillet over medium heat. Add bacon and fry until golden and slightly crisp, about 2 minutes. Drain all but 1 tbsp (15 mL) fat from wok. Add shallots, garlic, mushrooms, pumpkin and lotus root; sauté for 2 minutes. Add stock, soya sauce and oyster sauce; bring to a boil. Cover and cook 10 minutes or until vegetables are tender. Add green onions; stir to mix and cook 1 minute. Stir in dissolved cornstarch; bring to a boil and cook until sauce is slightly thickened. Season with salt and pepper. Serve.

# FIVE-SPICE AND SPINACH SCALLOPED POTATOES

**SERVES 4**

*This dish tastes best when it is allowed to cool completely and is later reheated for 20 minutes.*

*For a dramatic presentation, place a weight on the cooked casserole and refrigerate overnight. The next day, cut cubes from the casserole and reheat by pan-frying or baking to a golden brown.*

*For best results, cut the potatoes as thinly as possible, using a mandolin or vegetable slicer.*

**Buttered 12-inch square (3.5 L) casserole dish**
**Preheat oven to 350° F (180° C)**

| | | |
|---|---|---:|
| 3 cups | milk | 750 mL |
| 4 | thin slices ginger root | 4 |
| 4 | green onions, thinly sliced | 4 |
| 1 tsp | 5-spice powder | 5 mL |
| 1 tsp | salt | 5 mL |
| 1 tsp | freshly ground black pepper | 5 mL |
| 1 tbsp | minced garlic | 15 mL |
| 8 oz | spinach, washed and trimmed | 250 g |
| 1 tsp | sesame oil | 5 mL |
| 4 | large white potatoes, peeled and very thinly sliced | 4 |
| 2 cups | grated mozzarella cheese | 500 mL |

1. In a saucepan combine milk, ginger root, green onions, 5-spice powder, salt and pepper. Bring to a boil and immediately remove from heat. (The milk will triple in volume, so be careful not to let the pot overflow; constant stirring helps to stop the expansion.) Let mixture sit for 10 minutes, strain and reserve.

2. In a nonstick skillet, heat oil over high heat for 30 seconds. Add garlic, spinach and sesame oil; stir-fry until the spinach begins to soften and turn bright green, about 1 or 2 minutes. Transfer to a plate and allow to cool. Chop coarsely and set aside.

3. Cover bottom of buttered dish with a layer of potato slices. Sprinkle a little cheese on top, then add a thin layer of spinach and cover with some of the milk mixture. Repeat with remaining potato slices, spinach and cheese, ending with a layer of potato, reserving 1/4 cup (50 mL) cheese. Top with remaining milk and reserved cheese, ensuring that the mixture is covered with liquid. (Add more milk, if necessary.) Bake 45 minutes or until a knife easily penetrates the casserole.

4. Remove from oven and let sit for at least 15 minutes. The milk mixture will thicken as the casserole cools. Serve warm.

# MASHED POTATOES WITH GINGER GREEN ONION PESTO

*This dish is a true meeting of cultures. Mashed potatoes, North America's all-time favorite comfort food, is complemented by an Asian pesto.*

*For an elegant finishing touch, try adding pan-fried Chinese sausage, sliced mushrooms fried in butter or warm seafood (such as shredded crab, smoked salmon or lobster meat) just before serving.*

| | | |
|---|---|---|
| 2 lbs | potatoes, preferably Yukon Gold, peeled and cut into 1-inch (2.5 cm) cubes | 1 kg |
| 1 tsp | salt | 5 mL |
| 1 cup | milk | 250 mL |
| 4 tbsp | GINGER GREEN ONION PESTO (see recipe, page 35) | 60 mL |
| | Salt and pepper to taste | |

1. In a large saucepan, combine potatoes and salt; cover with cold water. Bring to a boil and cook for 15 to 20 minutes (or until the potatoes are easily crushed with a fork). Drain and return to pot. Mash potatoes with a potato masher or fork (or put through a ricer), eliminating as many lumps as possible.

2. Warm potatoes over medium heat for 1 minute. Add pesto and stir well. Add just enough milk to make the mixture smooth and stir thoroughly. Season to taste with salt and pepper; serve immediately.

# RICE

*Steaming bowls of rice are the perfect accompaniment to most of the dishes in this book. The secret of perfect rice is to let it sit, tightly covered, for 10 minutes after the heat has been turned off. Although brown and wild rice aren't really part of Chinese cuisine, we've included cooking instructions for these varieties since they're both highly nutritious and we feel they complement our dishes in a "New World" spirit.*

*Electronic rice cookers are a great invention: They cook and hold rice at exactly the right temperature. If you're lucky enough to own one, follow the manufacturer's instructions to make perfect rice.*

# STEAMED RICE

## TYPES AND QUANTITIES OF RICE

### Short-Grained Rice

| | | |
|---|---|---|
| 2 cups | short-grained rice | 500 mL |
| 2 1/2 cups | stock or water | 625 mL |
| 1 tsp | salt (optional) | 5 mL |

### Long-Grained Rice

| | | |
|---|---|---|
| 2 cups | long-grained rice | 500 mL |
| 3 1/2 cups | stock *or* water | 875 mL |
| 1 tsp | salt (optional) | 5 mL |

### Wild and Brown Rice:

| | | |
|---|---|---|
| 2 cups | wild or brown rice | 500 mL |
| 4 1/2 cups | stock *or* water | 1.125 L |
| 1 tsp | salt (optional) | 5 mL |

## COOKING METHODS

### Stove Top

1. In a pot with a tight-fitting lid, combine rice, stock or water and, if using, salt. Bring to a boil, uncovered, stirring occasionally.

2. Cover, reduce heat to low and cook 15 minutes. (If using wild or brown rice, cook 45 minutes.) Remove from heat and let sit, covered, for an additional 10 minutes.

### Microwave

1. In a casserole dish with a lid, combine rice, stock (or water) and salt. Microwave 5 minutes on high power.

2. Reduce power to 50%; cook an additional 10 minutes (wild or brown rice, 30 minutes). Allow to sit 10 minutes.

# VARIATIONS

The simple addition of seasonings to the water in which rice is cooked can greatly enhance its flavor. Here are a few of our suggestions, but feel free to use your imagination.

**Ginger Rice:** 1 tbsp (15 mL) shredded ginger

**Garlic Rice:** 1 tbsp (15 mL) shredded garlic

**Saffron Rice:** Pinch of saffron

**Tomato Rice:** Substitute water with tomato juice

**Coconut Rice:** Substitute half water with coconut milk

**Lemon Grass Rice:** Add a 1-inch (2.5 cm) piece of lemon grass, cut in half, to the cooking water. Remove before serving.

# SAUTÉED RICE WITH MIXED VEGETABLES AND HERBS

**SERVES 4**

*This rice stir-fry is a great base for many of our main-course dishes and makes a healthy meal by itself.*

*Feel free to add any fresh seasonal vegetable and, for a crunchy garnish, sprinkle sesame seeds or nuts on top.*

**Baking sheet**

| | | |
|---|---|---|
| 1 cup | short-grained rice | 250 mL |
| 4 cups | water | 1 L |
| 1 tbsp | vegetable oil | 15 mL |
| 1 tbsp | minced ginger root | 15 mL |
| 1 | red bell pepper, seeded and cut into 1/2-inch (1 cm) cubes | 1 |
| 2 | small zucchini, cut into 1/2-inch (1 cm) cubes | 2 |
| 1 cup | *sui choy* (Napa cabbage), finely chopped | 250 mL |
| 1 cup | corn kernels, fresh or frozen | 250 mL |
| 4 | green onions, thinly sliced | 4 |
| 1 tsp | sesame oil | 5 mL |
| 2 tbsp | minced basil | 25 mL |
| 1 tbsp | minced cilantro | 15 mL |
| | Salt and pepper to taste | |

1.  In a small saucepan, combine rice and water. Bring to a boil; cook 15 to 20 minutes, stirring occasionally, until the rice is tender. Drain, but do not rinse. Transfer rice to a baking sheet and spread out to cool.

2.  In a nonstick wok or skillet, heat oil for 45 seconds. Add ginger root, red pepper, zucchini, *sui choy*, corn and green onions. Sauté 3 to 4 minutes until vegetables are heated through.

3.  Add rice and season with sesame oil, basil and cilantro. Stir-fry 2 to 3 minutes to warm rice through. Season with salt and pepper, transfer to a warm platter and serve.

PEA TOPS WITH PANCETTA AND TOFU (PAGE 144)

# STEAMED RICE WITH GRAINY MUSTARD AND ORANGE PEEL

**SERVES 4 TO 6**

*The exotic combination of mustard and orange peel transforms ordinary rice into a real treat. This rice is wonderful with salmon, in particular, and any seafood in general.*

| 2 cups | long-grained rice | 500 mL |
|---|---|---|
| 3 1/2 cups | stock or water | 875 mL |
| 1 tsp | salt | 5 mL |
| 2 tbsp | grainy mustard | 25 mL |
| 1 | orange, juice and chopped zest | 1 |

1. In a pot with a tight-fitting lid, combine rice, stock or water, salt, mustard, orange juice and zest. Bring to a boil; cook, uncovered, stirring occasionally.

2. Cover pot tightly. Reduce heat to low and cook for 15 minutes. Remove from heat and let sit, with lid on, for an additional 10 minutes.

≺ CANDIED GINGER AND STRAWBERRY PARFAIT (PAGE 177)

# STEAMED RICE WITH COCONUT AND LEMON

*This rice is a great base for hot and spicy dishes.*

*There is no perfect substitute for coconut milk but if you can't find it, use 1/2 cup (125 mL) finely chopped coconut and increase the liquid to 3 1/2 cups (875 mL) of stock or water.*

| | | |
|---|---|---|
| 2 cups | long-grained rice | 500 mL |
| 2 1/2 cups | stock *or* water | 625 mL |
| 1 tsp | salt | 5 mL |
| 1 | can (14 oz [398 mL]) coconut milk | 1 |
| 1 | lemon, juice and zest | 1 |

1. In a pot with a tight-fitting lid, combine rice, stock or water, salt, coconut milk, lemon juice and zest. Bring to a boil; cook, uncovered, stirring occasionally.

2. Cover pot tightly. Reduce heat to low; cook for 15 minutes. Remove from heat and let sit, with lid on, for an additional 10 minutes.

# STICKY RICE WITH TOMATO JUICE, VEGETABLES AND GARLIC

*This satisfying dish is a simple and elegant way to feed a crowd or serve a great vegetarian main course.*

*The dense chunks of rice are stir-fried with vegetables and ginger into a colorful Chinese risotto.*

| | | |
|---|---|---|
| 1 1/2 cups | sticky (or short-grained) rice | 375 mL |
| 3 cups | tomato juice | 750 mL |
| 1 tsp | salt | 5 mL |
| 2 tbsp | vegetable oil | 25 mL |
| 2 tbsp | minced ginger root | 25 mL |
| 1 tsp | chili sauce | 5 mL |
| 1 | medium onion, cut into 1/2-inch (1 cm) dice | 1 |
| 1 | large red bell pepper, cut into 1/2-inch (1 cm) dice | 1 |
| 2 | small zucchini, cut into 1/2-inch (1 cm) dice | 2 |
| 1 tsp | sesame oil | 5 mL |
| | Salt and pepper to taste | |
| 2 | green onions, thinly sliced | 2 |
| | Toasted sesame seeds | |

1. In a saucepan combine rice, tomato juice and salt. Bring to a boil; cover tightly, reduce heat to low and cook 15 minutes. Remove from heat and let sit, tightly covered, for an additional 10 minutes.

2. In a nonstick wok or large skillet, heat oil on high for 30 seconds. Add ginger root, chili sauce, onion, red pepper and zucchini. Sauté 2 to 3 minutes until vegetables are heated through.

3. Add rice; season with sesame oil and salt and pepper. Stir-fry 4 to 6 minutes to heat the rice through. Scrape the rice from the sides of the wok with a wooden spoon or spatula to loosen the browned bits. Transfer to a warm platter and garnish with green onions and sesame seeds. Serve immediately.

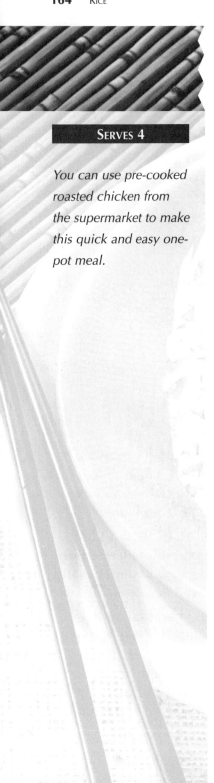

*You can use pre-cooked
roasted chicken from
the supermarket to make
this quick and easy one-
pot meal.*

# CHICKEN AND EGG FRIED RICE

| | | |
|---|---|---:|
| 1 1/2 tbsp | vegetable oil, divided | 20 mL |
| 3 | eggs, beaten | 3 |
| | Salt and pepper to taste | |
| 1 tbsp | minced ginger root | 15 mL |
| 2 | green onions, finely chopped | 2 |
| 2 cups | diced cooked chicken meat | 500 mL |
| 2 tbsp | chicken stock | 25 mL |
| 2 tbsp | finely chopped red bell peppers | 25 mL |
| 1/2 cup | frozen peas | 125 mL |
| 1/2 cup | canned corn kernels | 125 mL |
| 3 cups | cooked rice | 750 mL |
| | Salt and pepper to taste | |

1. In a nonstick wok or skillet, heat 1/2 tbsp (7 mL) oil over medium heat. Add eggs; cook to make a thin omelet by swirling the pan so the eggs flow onto as large a surface as possible. Season lightly with salt and pepper. Remove, chop coarsely and set aside.

2. Heat remaining oil in wok over medium heat. Add ginger root and onions; fry until fragrant, about 30 seconds. Add chicken, chicken stock, peppers, peas and corn; stir-fry 2 minutes. Add rice; stir-fry until well mixed and the grains are separated, about 2 minutes. Add eggs and stir to mix well. Season with salt and pepper; stir to mix. Serve immediately.

*This rice is meant to be served in combination with other dishes in a Chinese-style dinner. At Chinese restaurants, a similar recipe, made with the addition of diced chicken, is often served at the end of a banquet.*

# FRIED RICE WITH ANCHOVIES AND CILANTRO

| | | |
|---|---|---|
| 1 tbsp | vegetable oil | 15 mL |
| 4 | oil-packed anchovy fillets, finely chopped | 4 |
| 1 tbsp | minced ginger root | 15 mL |
| 3 cups | cooked rice | 750 mL |
| 1 tbsp | chicken stock | 15 mL |
| 1/4 cup | finely chopped cilantro | 50 mL |
| | Salt and pepper to taste | |

1. In a nonstick wok or skillet, heat oil over medium heat. Add anchovies and ginger root; fry until fragrant, about 30 seconds.

2. Add rice and stir-fry until the anchovy mixture is thoroughly integrated and the grains are separated, about 2 minutes. Add chicken stock; stir and cook until rice is heated through, about 1 minute. (Add more chicken stock if rice appears too dry.) Add cilantro; stir to combine. Season with salt and pepper; stir to mix. Serve immediately.

# LEEK AND BACON FRIED RICE

*Serve this as a side dish or add more ingredients — such as diced vegetables, meats or seafood — and make it a one-wok meal.*

*Leftover fried rice will taste just as good reheated in the microwave.*

| | | |
|---|---|---|
| 4 | strips bacon or pancetta, finely chopped | 4 |
| 1 | large whole leek, white and green parts separated and finely chopped | 1 |
| 3 cups | cooked rice | 750 mL |
| 1 tbsp | chicken stock | 15 mL |
| | Salt and pepper to taste | |

1. Heat a nonstick wok or skillet over medium heat. Add bacon and fry until golden and just beginning to turn brown, about 2 minutes. Add white part of leeks and stir-fry until wilted and fragrant, about 1 minute. Add green part of leeks and stir to mix thoroughly.

2. Add rice to mixture; stir-fry until well combined and the grains are separated, about 2 minutes. Add chicken stock; cook, stirring, for 1 minute or until the rice is heated through. (Add more stock if the rice appears too dry.) Season with salt and pepper; stir to mix. Serve immediately.

**SERVES 4**

*This simple fried rice
makes a wonderful
accompaniment to
savory dishes such as
PAN-ROASTED TILAPIA
(see recipe, page 92) or
PAN-FRIED PORK CHOPS
WITH SUN-DRIED
TOMATOES AND CILANTRO
(see recipe, page 138).*

# EGG AND SCALLION FRIED RICE

| | | |
|---|---|---|
| 1 tbsp | vegetable oil, divided | 15 mL |
| 3 | eggs, beaten | 3 |
| | Salt and pepper to taste | |
| 1 tbsp | minced ginger root | 15 mL |
| 2 | green onions, finely chopped | 2 |
| 2 tbsp | chicken stock | 25 mL |
| 2 tbsp | red bell pepper, finely chopped | 25 mL |
| 3 cups | cooked rice | 750 mL |
| | Salt and pepper to taste | |

1.  In a nonstick wok or large skillet, heat 1/2 tbsp (7 mL) oil over medium heat. Add eggs and cook to make a thin omelet by swirling the pan so the eggs flow onto as large a surface as possible. Season lightly with salt and pepper. Remove, chop coarsely and set aside.

2.  Heat remaining oil in wok over medium heat. Add ginger root and onions; stir-fry until fragrant, about 30 seconds. Add stock and red pepper; stir briefly. Add rice; stir-fry until well mixed and the grains are separated, about 2 minutes. Add omelet pieces and stir to mix well. Season with salt and pepper; stir to mix. Serve immediately.

# DESSERTS

# BAKED CANDIED PECANS

**Preheat oven to 275° F (140° C)**

**Baking sheet sprayed with vegetable spray**

| | | |
|---|---|---|
| 1 lb | shelled raw pecan or walnut halves | 500 g |
| 1 cup | water | 250 mL |
| 1 cup | sugar | 250 mL |
| 1/2 cup | honey | 125 mL |
| 1/4 tsp | salt | 1 mL |
| 2 tbsp | toasted sesame seeds (optional) | 25 mL |

1. In large skillet, combine water, sugar, honey and salt. Bring to a boil; cook until liquid coats the back of a spoon with the consistency of corn syrup. Reduce heat to medium. Add nuts; stir and boil for about 1 minute, making sure that nuts are well coated.

2. With a slotted spoon, transfer nuts to prepared baking sheet. (Be sure to separate and spread them out evenly.) Bake 20 to 25 minutes or until golden brown, turning once.

3. Remove from oven and cool slightly. If you want to eat the nuts as a snack, while they're still warm and sticky, toss them in a mixing bowl with sesame seeds. Spread out coated nuts again on baking sheet sheet; let cool and harden thoroughly. Store in a glass jar with a tight-fitting lid.

**MAKES ABOUT 2 CUPS (500 mL)**

In Chinese cuisine, these popular New Year candied snacks were traditionally made with walnuts because they signify togetherness and are supposedly good for one's brains. We opted to use pecans because they are easier to handle, but you can make them with walnuts if you wish.

If using walnuts, bring 4 cups (1 L) water to a boil. Add walnuts and blanch for 2 minutes. Remove from heat; drain well, pat dry and proceed with recipe.

These nuts can be served alone as a snack or as a garnish in other dishes such as YARD-LONG BEAN SALAD (see recipe, page 73) or ORANGE GINGER GARLIC BEEF (see recipe, page 126).

*This easy ice cream dessert is simple and addictive. To crush candied pecans, pulse in a food processor until a coarse grainy consistency is achieved.*

# CANDIED PECAN COFFEE TARTUFO

| | | |
|---|---|---|
| 1/4 cup | crushed BAKED CANDIED PECANS (see recipe, facing page) | 50 mL |
| 2 tbsp | very finely ground espresso coffee | 25 mL |
| 2 pints | coffee ice cream, removed from freezer 5 minutes before using | 1 L |

1. On a plate, mix pecans and coffee; set aside.
2. Using an extra-large scoop (or even a ladle), scoop out 4 to 6 ice cream balls. Roll them in the nut mixture until well-coated and serve immediately.

# GINGER PANNA COTTA WITH MANGO

**SERVES 6 TO 8**

*The cherished flavors of mango and ginger — and the rich, silky texture reminiscent of those popular Chinese egg custard tarts — combine here to make a perfect Chinese-Italian fusion dessert. We've suggested mango, since it's a Chinese favorite, but you can also use fruits and berries, in season, such as apricots, peaches, strawberries, raspberries or blueberries.*

| | | |
|---|---|---:|
| 1 | envelope unflavored gelatin | 1 |
| 4 tbsp | water | 60 mL |
| 1 cup | granulated sugar | 250 mL |
| 1 cup | milk | 250 mL |
| 1 | can (14 oz [398 mL]) evaporated milk | 1 |
| 1 cup | whipping (35%) cream | 250 mL |
| 1 tbsp | minced ginger root | 15 mL |
| 2 | mangoes, peeled and diced | 2 |

1.  In a large heavy-bottomed saucepan, sprinkle gelatin over water. Let sit for 2 minutes, then stir until gelatin has dissolved. Add sugar, milk, cream and ginger root; cook over low heat, stirring constantly, until the mixture boils, about 5 minutes. Remove from heat, stir in evaporated milk and allow to rest for 2 minutes to blend flavors.

2.  Strain mixture into dessert bowls. When cool, cover with plastic wrap and refrigerate until firm, 6 hours or overnight. To serve, top each portion with a generous amount of diced fruit.

# BAKED WONTONS STUFFED WITH APPLES AND CINNAMON

SERVES 4

*These tasty treats (which can also be made with pears, bananas, pineapple, blueberries or raspberries) are virtually fat-free, simple to make and cook quickly.*

*Be sure to chop the fruit finely; otherwise, the wonton wrappers won't fit together properly.*

**Preheat oven to 350° F (180° C)**

| | | |
|---|---|---|
| 12 | round wonton wrappers | 12 |
| 1 | egg, beaten | 1 |
| 2 | apples, peeled and finely diced | 1 |
| 2 tbsp | brown sugar | 25 mL |
| 1/2 tsp | ground cinnamon | 2 mL |
| | Granulated sugar for garnish | |

1. In a small bowl, combine apple, brown sugar and cinnamon; mix thoroughly.

2. On a clean flat surface, lay out 6 wonton wrappers. Brush with beaten egg. Place 1 heaping tbsp (15 to 17 mL) of the apple mixture on each wrapper. Lay a second wrapper on top of the mixture and, using your fingertips, press lightly to remove the trapped air. Press the edges together to seal. Brush with egg and sprinkle sugar on top.

3. Bake in preheated oven 10 to 12 minutes or until golden. Remove from the oven and dust with additional sugar, if desired. Serve warm.

# MAPLE CUSTARD RICE PUDDING

*Baked rice custard is a favorite Chinese treat, usually served with dim sum meals. North Americans also consider custard a great comfort food. This particular version is delicious hot or cold and achieves its distinctiveness with the addition of maple syrup.*

*For a slightly creamier consistency, cook in a hot water bath 40 to 45 minutes.*

**Preheat oven to 325° F (160° C)**

**12-inch square (3.5 L) casserole dish, buttered**

| | | |
|---|---|---:|
| 3 cups | milk | 750 mL |
| 3 cups | light (10%) cream | 750 mL |
| 1 tsp | vanilla extract | 5 mL |
| 1/2 cup | maple syrup | 125 mL |
| 6 | large eggs | 6 |
| 2 cups | cooked long-grain rice | 500 mL |
| | Maple syrup to taste | |

1. In a large bowl, combine milk, cream, vanilla, maple syrup and eggs; mix well to ensure that the egg is thoroughly incorporated. Add rice and stir to combine thoroughly.

2. Pour mixture into prepared dish; bake 30 to 40 minutes in preheated oven until the top is golden and bubbling and the mixture is set. Serve warm or cold, drizzled with maple syrup to taste.

# CARAMELIZED PEAR OATMEAL SESAME CRUMBLE

**SERVES 4**

*Caramelized pear and a topping laced with sesame seeds and scented with almond flavoring give a new spin to fruit crumble. Apples also work well in this recipe.*

**Preheat oven to 350° F (180° C)**
**9-inch square (2.5 L) baking dish**

## Caramelized Pear

| | | |
|---|---|---|
| 1 cup | granulated sugar | 250 mL |
| 1/2 cup | water | 125 mL |
| 1 tbsp | honey | 15 mL |
| 2 tbsp | butter | 25 mL |
| 1 lb | pears, peeled and cut into 1/2-inch (1 cm) dice | 500 g |

## Crumble

| | | |
|---|---|---|
| 1 cup | flour | 250 mL |
| 1 cup | brown sugar | 250 mL |
| 1 cup | quick-cook oatmeal | 250 mL |
| 1 tsp | salt | 5 mL |
| 4 tbsp | sesame seeds | 60 mL |
| 4 tbsp | melted butter | 60 mL |
| 1 tsp | almond extract | 5 mL |

1. In a large wok or skillet, combine sugar, water and honey. Cook over high heat until mixture thickens and begins to darken at the edges, about 15 minutes. Add butter; swirl pan to distribute. The caramel should darken to a deep brown. Add diced pears and toss until well-coated. (The caramel will lump together at this point, but will dissolve with further cooking.) Set aside.

2. In a large bowl, combine flour, brown sugar, oatmeal, salt and sesame seeds; mix well. Add melted butter and almond extract; mix thoroughly.

3. Spread caramelized pears over the bottom of baking dish. Spread topping over the pear mixture and bake in preheated oven for 30 minutes or until the top is golden and the juices are bubbling. The crumble can be served hot or cold, or cooled and reheated just before serving.

# COCONUT JELLY SQUARES

*This popular dim sum item makes a wonderfully simple everyday dessert. Try serving it with FRUIT SALAD WITH GINGER AND HONEY (see recipe, page 178) or jazz it up with some raspberry purée — just purée fresh or frozen (but thawed) raspberries in a blender until liquefied; add sugar to taste.*

**6-inch (15 cm) square dish for molding the jelly**

| | | |
|---|---|---|
| 1 | envelope unflavored gelatin | 1 |
| 1/2 cup | granulated sugar, divided | 125 mL |
| 1/2 cup | boiling water | 125 mL |
| 1 | can (14 oz [398 mL]) coconut milk | 1 |
| 1/2 cup | grated dried coconut | 125 mL |
| | Sugar to taste | |

1. In a mixing bowl, combine gelatin and 2 tbsp (25 mL) sugar. Add water and stir until gelatin is dissolved.

2. Add coconut milk and remaining sugar; mix well. (If desired, add more sugar to taste.) Pour mixture into mold and refrigerate until set, approximately 2 hours.

3. To serve: Dip the mold briefly in hot water to loosen contents and invert onto a flat working surface. Cut jelly into 1 1/2-inch (4 cm) squares. Spread dried coconut on a plate; thoroughly coat both sides of each jelly square. Serve squares on a platter by themselves or accompanied by raspberry purée or FRUIT SALAD WITH GINGER AND HONEY (see recipe, page 178).

# CANDIED GINGER AND STRAWBERRY PARFAIT

**SERVES 6**

*Frozen strawberries can be used if fresh ones are out of season. Be sure to check sweetness before adding honey as some frozen berries may already have sugar added.*

*Candied ginger is usually sold in a jar with syrup, but we have seen it in semi-dried form, coated in sugar. If that's the kind you're using, substitute ginger juice and honey for the syrup.*

*To make ginger juice: In a food processor or chopper, purée 8 thick slices of ginger root and 1 tbsp (15 mL) water. Extract juice by pushing pulp through a very fine sieve.*

| | | |
|---|---|---|
| 2 tbsp | minced candied ginger | 25 mL |
| 1 tsp | ginger juice (see note, at left) | 5 mL |
| 1 tbsp | syrup from candied ginger *or* 1 tbsp (15 mL) ginger juice, sweetened with 1 tsp (5 mL) honey | 15 mL |
| 2 cups | sliced strawberries | 500 mL |
| | Maple syrup, to taste | |
| 2 cups | vanilla ice cream | 500 mL |
| 1 cup | whipped cream | 250 mL |

1. In a bowl combine ginger, ginger juice, syrup and strawberries; mix well. Adjust sweetness with maple syrup and set aside to marinate for 20 minutes.

2. To serve: Place about 2 tbsp (25 mL) strawberry mixture in the bottom of a parfait glass. Add 2 tbsp (25 mL) ice cream; repeat layers until parfait glass is filled. Top with a dollop of whipped cream and serve immediately.

# FRUIT SALAD WITH GINGER AND HONEY

*The Chinese love simple fruit desserts. In Asia, a dessert called "icy bowls" (which resembles this fruit salad), is served over shaved ice, sometimes topped with coconut milk.*

*Feel free to add or substitute any fruits of your choice. Canned Asian fruits such as lychee and jackfruit will work very well in this recipe. And, of course, you can enrich it with coconut milk, if desired.*

## Sauce

| | | |
|---|---|---|
| 1/4 cup | honey | 50 mL |
| 1 tsp | lime zest | 5 mL |
| 1 tsp | orange zest | 5 mL |
| 2 tsp | minced ginger root | 10 mL |
| 1 cup | apples cut into 1-inch (2.5 cm) cubes | 250 mL |
| 1 cup | cantaloupe cut into 1-inch (2.5 cm) cubes | 250 mL |
| 2 cups | honeydew melon cut into 1-inch (2.5 cm) cubes | 500 mL |
| 1 cup | pineapple cut into 1-inch (2.5 cm) cubes | 250 mL |
| 1 cup | seedless red grapes | 250 mL |

1. In a small bowl or pot, combine sauce ingredients; heat 30 seconds in microwave or until warmed through on top of stove. Set aside to cool.

2. In a mixing bowl, combine fruits; add sauce and mix well. Serve plain or with ice cream or, if desired, with COCONUT JELLY SQUARES (see recipe, page 176).

# INDEX